The Enneagram of Society

Healing the Soul
to Heal the World

Books by Claudio Naranjo

Character and Neurosis: An Integrative View

The Divine Child and the Hero:
Inner Meaning in Children's Literature

The End of Patriarchy
and the Dawning of a Tri-une Society

Ennea-type Structures:
Self-Analysis for the Seeker

Enneatypes in Psychotherapy

Gestalt Therapy: The Attitude and Practice
of an Atheoretical Experientialism

The Healing Journey

How to Be

The One Quest

The Psychology of Meditation

Techniques of Gestalt Therapy

Transformation Through Insight:
Enneatypes in Life,
Literature and Clinical Practice

The Way of Silence
and the Talking Cure

Claudio Naranjo, M.D.

The Enneagram of Society

Healing the Soul to Heal the World

English translation by Paul Barnes

Gateways Books and Tapes
Nevada City, California

Published by:
Gateways Books and Tapes
P.O. Box 370
Nevada City, CA 95959
www.gatewaysbooksandtapes.com

First published in Spain under the title: *El Eneagrama de la Sociedad—
Males del Mundo, Males del Alma*, Temas de Hoy, 1995; Editorial La
Llave edition, 2000.
Translated from the Spanish by Paul Barnes.

ISBN: 0-89556-159-X

  Library of Congress Cataloging-in-Publication Data

  Naranjo, Claudio.
  [Eneagrama de la sociedad. English]
  The enneagram of society / Claudio Naranjo.
     p. cm.
  ISBN 0-89556-159-X
  1. Enneagram. 2. Deadly sins--Psychology. 3. Enneagram--
Social aspects. I. Title.
  BF698.35.E54N3813 2004
  155.26--dc22
                    2003026203

Contents

For Suzy, who lovingly put my dictation on paper.

Foreword to the 1995 Spanish edition

The publishers Temas de Hoy have put me right on the spot by asking me to introduce this book by Doctor Claudio Naranjo, an eminent psychiatrist and professor who moves like a pendulum between Chile and California. How could I, totally ignorant in the doctrine of Christian esoterics and the Enneagram, write something presentable about a book that has this doctrine as its nerve center? Without knowing what I was doing, I took on the commitment. But, morally obliged by my ignorance, I would not have hesitated to go back on the commitment if I had not discovered in these pages a thesis to whose resolution I have dedicated some attention and a goal with which I feel intimately comfortable.

The thesis: that during our century humanity has lived and continues to live in the midst of a profound historical crisis. A thesis that is, in addition, more than obvious: "The fact that we are in planetary crisis is self-evident," says Dr. Naranjo's first words in the prologue to his book. In a recent book of mine, entitled *Hope in a Time of Crisis*, I have attempted to sketch the general outlines of this prolonged crisis, and I have shown how nine prominent European thinkers have meanwhile conserved their historical hope. Each one, according to his or her own way of seeing and understanding, has put forth guidelines for individual life and collective life to reorder the world. While they do not plan for a paradise—an intrinsically utopian goal—they do envision a more satisfactory life than this to and fro progress from one hot war to another, and then another cold war, and at the end of that, with the living memory of millions of dead, genocides, concentration camps, and the crushing of the adversary, a world in which we find ourselves as needful of historical tranquility in the present and of reasonable faith in what is to come as we did before such a long, atrocious experience. What shall we do then? Definitively despair? Throw in the towel, and, if one has one's own plot of land, lock oneself up in it and just cultivate it? The nine thinkers I contemplated died with the clear awareness that their respective proposals, all noble and reasonable, many of which are frankly attractive, had failed. Some, it is true, accepted them, but the world did not; which did not prevent those with hope from preserving their faith in man until the end of their days. They did not see human existence—betraying its own truth is how one of them proposed defining it—as a useless passion. Many other names could have figured among them: one of these, that of Dr. Naranjo.

The goal: to get everyone with professional skills, each one according to his or her own possibilities, to contribute to the universal task of building a more acceptable historical world than the present one. How does the author of this book do this? Claudio Naranjo is a psychiatrist and a fervent devotee of the "Christian esoterics" that he discovered one day: "I can say," he states, "that [with this discovery] I was truly born and I entered into a new phase of my life, inspired and directed from beyond what I had known until then about myself." From there, he derives his desire to help others and to contribute to correcting what he calls "ills of the world." His starting point is the description of the nine enneatypes that may be distinguished in the ethical aberrations of the individual psyche. He then goes on to sketch the corresponding nine individual characters that are to be observed in our species and to present the nine modalities that can be distinguished in the substance of human love. Finally, on the basis of these three series of anthropological analyses, he presents the nine "ills of the world" to us, the most important social ailments that nowadays corrupt collective life. In short, he shows the ethical disturbances of individual life, makes us see how they are all realized socially, and invites each individual to try to better the world by knowing and by improving him or herself. To put it another way: with not merely cognitive, but also practical and uplifting intention, to aspire, in a present-day way, to fulfilling the *nosce te ipsum* of the ancient Greco-Latin world.

I read recently that when he was young, with the desire to contribute with struggles, not just with words, to the progress of humanity, Wittgenstein left the city, moved to a small mining village, and founded a primary school there for adults. "What I want is to improve the world," said one of his pupils. "So start by improving yourself," the philosopher replied. Dr. Claudio Naranjo says the same on the last page of his book: "If we consider it difficult for a healthy society to exist without the foundation of healthy individuals, it becomes imperative to recognize the political value of individual transformation." Even though this, he adds, is so poorly supported in so many cases by official institutions. With great intellectual finesse, exquisite sensitivity, and an extensive display of knowledge, this is the aim the author seeks in this book. He very clearly tells us: "...think about all that will be added unto us if we first of all occupy the kingdom that is to be found within our hearts." I sincerely join him in his wish.

—Professor Pedro Laín Entralgo
Member, Spanish Royal Academy

Foreword to the Latin American Edition

"What I see, mainly, is that materialism is not enough for the vast majority of people. They are seeking something else."

–Georges Duby
An 1000 an 2000. Sur les traces de nos peurs

Humanity finds itself once more under the sign of a great change. As in all threshold processes, hope here again awakens intense self-reflection, both individual and collective. Even so, all sincere, deep reflection is inevitably accompanied by disappointments. Some of these are directly proportional to the magnitude of the time frame, which in this case is on the order of the millennium.

In the cycles of human life, midday seldom fulfills the promises of the dawn. The twentieth century, launched under the aegis of the unlimited belief in progress, with its yearning to transform the world, presents a disheartening retrospective: almost two hundred million dead in wars, local conflicts, terrorist attacks, and other forms of systematic aggression, linked to crime in its diverse vicissitudes.

Throughout the past century, innumerable modalities of violence have arisen. Many of these are visible, such as social exclusion and the dismantling of ecosystems, both on an unprecedented scale. Others, though less conspicuous—for example, the dismantling of institutions, the dilution of local and regional identities, the progressive erosion of the intermediate bodies of society, the dissolution of national states (due to fragmentation or supranational integration), the shuffling of ethnic frontiers, the draining of substance from beliefs, rites, and values—are of no lesser importance.

Who, and how many, will become the victims of this massive disenchantment with the perspectives of salvation brought on by the technological, scientific, aesthetic, and moral conquests of the modern world? The hundreds of millions of people deprived of material comfort, for whom the welfare state has been but yet another unfulfilled promise of the modern world? Undoubtedly, if one gives credit to the words of Ortega y Gasset, who contends that it is only possible to be happy in the manner of one's own epoch, those excluded from consuming in a consumer society contribute decisively to the critical mass of the frustrated and afflicted, yielding increasing unease, with no other remedy than the always doubtful effect of social policies.

This society, however, has not managed to please those who, on the other hand, are lavished with all comforts. On the contrary, its most obvious beneficiaries are just another category of wretches. Victims in a wider, more subtle and indiscriminate sense of exclusion, the apparently well-off also end up as members of the angst-ridden, resentful, suffering, restless, inattentive, inhibited, taciturn, lonely, somber, and frivolous multitude of unsatisfied people, since despite their material affluence, they lead their lives deficient in inner comfort. They are virtually prisoners of an existence deprived of indispensable moral plenitude and hence lacking any deeper meaning.

The Millennium with its anxieties, fears, and hopes is inevitably a time of questions about ends and beginnings, about the meaning and destiny of human life—an appropriate epoch therefore to seek once more answers to the big question: What is Man? What is human life?

Mircea Eliade declared that the "center" of every culture is the concept of life. The most diverse societies, distinct and distant in time and space, surprisingly coincide in this sense. Food, fertility and protection against enemies, illnesses and hunger are merely part of life. Subsistence, physical health and offspring, maybe prosperity or wealth, though necessary, have never seemed sufficient to man to guarantee an adequate life.

Human beings in all epochs and cultures have conceived a broader project. We might call it the search for a full life. To achieve this, demographic vigor, material abundance, shelter from the elements and protection against misfortune was not enough. The idea of fullness implies, moreover, and perhaps above all, a vigorous longevity, not only of the body, but also of the spirit, in both this and the other world.

This is the idea of life as we may encounter it in the Vedic texts, contained in the category of amrita, and in the Nahuatl mythology, where it is embodied in the divine character Quetzalcoatl, and even in certain African cosmologies, which circumscribe it by the notion of axé. In all of these, vitality is conceived of as a gradient. Life is something that one has more or less. Descendents, prosperity, physical health, good fortune, and encouraging prospects, on a social and spiritual level, make it tend towards fullness. A lack in any of these diverse dimensions leads to decadence, thus jeopardizing the most daring of human yearnings, the possible permanence of existence.

During the second half of the nineteenth century, throughout heated discussions, the founding fathers of modern social thought scientifically legitimized the thesis of the psychological unity of the human species. Then, the French school of sociology, under the aegis of Durkheim and Mauss, established the conviction that all social facts are psychological facts, representations that are present in the individual or collective consciousness.

These domains, though distinct, are thus presented as being interconnected, a condition which gives rise, in the sphere of anthropological reflection, to the entire problem of the relations between individuals and society. And, within that sphere arises the question as to the nature of these relations, the polemic between the sociogenesis and psychogenesis of social facts; the question as to the construction of subjectivity and consequently the discussion with respect to personality and its links to social structure and culture, a rich vein, explored by American Culturalists.

These considerable efforts, on different fronts and with varied strategies, have not managed, however, to dispel the existing relations of indetermination in the center of this polarity. Between this pair of opposites there undoubtedly exists a current of tension, perhaps it would be better to say ad-tension. That is, a tension of consciousness aimed, like a beam of light, at the other pole.

It is sometimes as if the avatar of an ancient and powerful metaphor were irresistibly drawing us, maintaining us, still, under its spell. Macrocosmos and microcosmos. What are the mutual correspondences? Who serves as a model to whom? Social construction of the persona, or personae constructing the social universe? To whom does primacy belong?

The positive appraisal of creativity, so notable among modern people, would lead us to believe in the effective existence of personal freedom. And, even so, discursive insistence seems more like the search for a counterweight for the enormous, anonymous constraints that individuals are subject to in present-day society

In fact, among the innumerable inventions of the twentieth century, one finds a whole battery of resources, elaborated by different social authorities, or sometimes under their auspices, to mold the hearts and minds of their constituents: conditioned reflexes, brain washing, psychological warfare, subliminal influence, control of the imagination, behavioral engineering, directed information, instantaneous hypnosis, and neurolinguistic programming. Thanks to the development and constant expansion of these paraphernalia, the Brazilian philosopher Olavo de Carvalho concludes that the twentieth century was not noteworthy so much for ideology, atomic physics, or computing, but rather for the "omnipresence of mind manipulation, in contemporary life," a fact that suggests a disturbing question: Isn't it more probable [than the conservation intact of intuitive, evaluating faculties] that humanity thus manipulated, idiotized, mocked twenty-four hours a day, ends up entering into a state of chronic self-deception?

Without of course overlooking how many lies mankind has been told on a planetary scale, we must not forget that men also lie with respect to themselves, not only to others, but above all to themselves. They are therefore accomplices in some way, when not followers, of the universal cult of self-deception, given over to the perverse ritual of their neuroses, of which they are at one and the same time victims, due to suffering their consequences, and executioners, due to feeding them. And this appears to be the true source of all the dramas of existence, in accordance with which the vast majority of human beings remain condemned to what Emerson called "a life of quiet desperation."

Dr. Claudio Naranjo has put all his erudition, his sensitivity, his therapeutic competence, and his energy into perfecting an effective antidote against this not always mute desperation. *The Enneagram of Society: Healing the Soul to Heal the World* is the recent fruit of an entire lifetime dedicated to what is, without doubt, the greatest and most perennial of adventures: inner conquest; knowledge, and mastery of oneself.

This exquisite book once more presents the algorithm of characterology that came to the West in Gurdjieff's baggage in 1917, and which has come to be known since then under the name of the Enneagram, a device for self-knowledge. Naranjo makes decisive contributions, both in conceptual terms and in applications of a therapeutic nature.

This time, however, the work is not only consecrated to the hermeneutics of this map of ethical aberrations of the individual human soul. Beyond their peculiarities, he considers them within the sphere of amorous relationships, a paradigmatic expression of this anthropological universe that is the beginning of reciprocity. Not content with this however, Claudio Naranjo closes the book with an essay of social criticism, taking psychopathologies of the individual character—maladies of the soul—as a privileged viewpoint for identifying their counterparts on a social level—maladies of the world.

His argument, which is masterly in its execution and daring, has everything necessary to attract the attention not only of those who are interested (on their own behalf or that of others) in the secrets of the human soul, but also of those who are devotees of symbolic objects from an anthropological viewpoint. The latter, especially, will be able, thanks to this book by Dr. Naranjo, to consider and discuss very provocative hypotheses. One of these, surely the most daring, is that in the case of the Enneagram, we find ourselves face to face with a general tool for organizing human experience, face to face with a type of anthropological universal. The other hypothesis proposes that on the basis of the Enneagram we reconsider a possible homology between man and his social universe.

Whatever the findings and conclusions of this research may be, *The Enneagram of Society*, rather than material for active speculation, presents us with an invitation to rebuild the world, starting with our own transformation into beings capable of assuming responsibility for our own acts, both outer and inner, a condition essential to any leap into self-transcendence, and thus crucial to the search for the ideal of a full life.

—Arno Vogel
Rio de Janeiro, 4th December 2000

Arno Vogel is the Director of the Latin American Faculty for Sociology (FLACO). This Foreword is from the Dolmen Publishing edition, Santiago, Chile.

Author's Preface

It is obvious that we currently find ourselves in a planetary crisis. To deny this, you have to be either blind or a messianic visionary for whom the future is already present.

But it is best for us not to think like this. Nor does it serve us to neglect what is crucial to us. It has been said, "God helps those who help themselves."

What then are we to do? This book proposes the following:

1. Work towards our spiritual progress.

2. Cultivate the love that shines both towards the other and towards the self, the love which is found in the sphere of I/you—by working towards healthy interpersonal relationships.

3. Become aware of the ego, the illness or infection of "sin" that comes down to us through the generations—the visages of the accusing, fictitious Adversary—so as to be able to shield ourselves from its temptation.

4. To become aware of the reverberations of the psychopathology of character in the society that we have created, in order to be able to triumph over the lethal inertia of institutions.

This book came into being as a result of the invitation of the Spanish publishing house *Temas de Hoy* to write something from the perspective of a "cosmic map" of Christian esotericism that has recently come to light: the Enneagram.

Apart from suggesting in the sub-title that the core of the ills of the world lies in the ills of the soul, I deal with a fourfold topic: sins, character neuroses, the aberrations of love, and the pathologies of society.

The book is divided into four parts:

a) A presentation of the enneagram as a map of the ills, sins, or fundamental passions of the individual psyche, as well as the relationships between sins and pathologies.

b) A more detailed description of personality disorders or character neuroses that derive from each of these.

c) A discussion of the disturbances of love that each human character entails.

d) A contemplation of a possible "enneagram of society" —an essay of social criticism from the viewpoint of the psychopathologies of the individual character.

For many years now, I have moved between continents at the rhythm of the whale, and when I am in Berkeley I draw a circle around me to make myself—if not invisible—as little visible as possible, so as to be able to bring out from inside me a series of books. These books have been writing themselves in my mind, and I did not wish to deny them their birth through intentional negligence. Thankfully, I have found that the four months of my planned stay at home (before leaving once more on a teaching-therapy tour of South America) have been enough to write this book.

It was a rapid, gratifying process. *The Enneagram of Society—Healing the Soul to Heal the World* was born one day in November when Ymelda Navajo, as I have already mentioned, invited me to write something on the Enneagram and Personality. I proposed a very brief book, a somewhat expanded transcription of a talk I had just given at the University of Deusto (in the Basque

Country) on "the ills of the world in the light of the ills of love." In contrast, she proposed that I also talk about characters. And in view of this it seemed appropriate to begin the volume with an introductory treatise on the ills of the soul—whether they be called sins or pathologies. And here it is!

This book has not only turned out to be especially easy to write, in parallel with some more modest projects, but also has turned out to be severe. I hope that in exchange for losing some readers who would prefer something lighter and more entertaining, its bare precision—unlubricated by any considerations—may be of use to the "inhabitants of purgatory," implicit knowers of the "conscious suffering" that is indispensable on that path of purification that separates us from the Supreme.

—Claudio Naranjo

I

Passions, Pathologies and Neurotic Motivations

Practically every culture has its legend of paradise: the idea of having "fallen" from a better life condition, of having lost a state of original or primordial happiness and harmony.

Whether the idea of a paradise at the beginning of our history is true or not, there is some sense in thinking of paradise as a principle outside of time, a mythical *illo tempore* with respect to which our neurotic state constitutes a fall.

Western religion has spoken to us of the fall as the consequence of a sin, and has correspondingly spoken to us of redemption through the purification of our sins. Original sin, however, is not only that which has come down to us from original times by means of an emotional plague (or karmic continuity) through the generations. Two notions overlap in the notion of original sin: the idea of transmittable sin and the *principle* of sin, its "source" in the special sense of principle (*arché*) or fundament—an *essence* of the fall beyond the diverse manifestations of awareness in its exile from paradise.

Saint Augustine said of this meta-sin that original sin consists of an aspect of *ignorantia* and another of *dificultas*. Today, we would translate this as: a disorder of awareness and an interference with action. A non explicit element in this Augustinian dichotomy, though one commonly understood as an essential aspect of sin, is what theologians (such as the Venerable Bede) called "concupiscence"—equivalent to what Buddhists have also seen at the heart of sin: a hyper-desire (*trishna*, attachment).

Little is said nowadays in the modern lay world concerning "sin," and those who still preserve the term in their vocabulary are suspected of being traditionalists or guilt-ridden. On the other hand, much is said of pathologies. We apply the language of medicine to the problem of consciousness, and by doing so we inadvertently rescue the original sense of the word sin that had almost been forgotten after the contamination of the notion of wrongness as a dysfunction with that of wrongness as evil.

The psychiatric perspective has invited us to think not so much of evil acts or destructive behavior as of dysfunctions, confusions or deviations of the impulses. And it is in this last term that we find the original meaning of *hamarteia*—a borrowed term from archery used to designate sin in the gospels, and whose original meaning was not hitting the target.

Here, original theology meets with today's psychopathology, because since Freud we also understand the faults of the psyche as deviations of energy—impediments that interpose themselves between spontaneity and action, causing an overflow of psychic energy towards secondary ends.

The difference between sins and pathologies is, however, the *locus* of responsibility: in so far as "sin" accuses, making the individual responsible, "pathology" excuses, making past or present causes beyond the individual himself responsible. While we are *victims* of mental and interpersonal pathologies, we are *responsible* for our sins.

Obviously, each of these perspectives has its use and thus they complement one another, since we are at the same time physical beings subject to a causal universe, and beings—more than animals—made responsible by a spark of freedom.

Is it appropriate then to talk about certain basic aberrations of psychic life—call them sins or pathologies?

The Christian tradition replies affirmatively, and offers us its teaching with respect to the capital sins—differentiated forms of expression of the single sin that are at the head (*caput*) of all that we can do wrong in our relationship with others, with life, and with ourselves.

What then are such sins?

While pathologies have been described by psychology mainly as constellations of symptoms or characteristics that belong to the sphere of *action* ("character traits"), sins such as pride or envy point towards the sphere of *motivation*.

We may say that these are destructive desires, exaggerated desires—"passions"—even when they are sometimes not forms of attraction but rather of repulsion, and some may be described as a passion for being dispassionate. Love gives, while passions constitute forms of insatiability: a neurotic need cannot be satisfied except transitorily, because deep down it demands something that doesn't exist. Carefully considered, the passions reveal themselves to be a thirst for Being, ultimately based on a loss of contact with the Being—i.e., spiritual confusion.

It is clear that the doctrine of the seven capital sins (as well as that of the Trinity) is not to be found in the gospels. Scholars believe that they both reached the heart of Christianity through the Hellenistic cultural context in which early Christianity developed and in which spiritual doctrines from Babylonian esotericism survived. Yet although we find no systematic mention in the gospels of the seven sins, we do find them (with the greedy as the "inebriated" and the lustful as "fornicators") even before the gospels were written—in one of the epistles of Horace[1], each in relation to a particular antidote.

> *Fervet avaritia miseroque cupidine pectus:*
> *Sunt verba et voces, quibus hunc lenire dolorem*
> *Possis, et magnam morbi deponere partem.*
> *Laudis amore tumes: sunt certa piacula, quae te*
> *Ter pure lecto poterunt recreare libello.*
> *Invidus, iracundus, iners, vinosus, amator,*
> *Nemo adeo ferus est ut non mitescere possit*
> *Si modo culturae patientem commodet aurem.*

[The human heart burns with avarice and miserable thirst; there are words and formulas to calm this suffering and to cure, at least in part, this ill. You are bloated with vanity: there are certain expiations that can revive you if you read a certain book three times precisely. The envious, angry, indolent, inebriated, sensual—none is so savage as not to be able to be tamed, as long as they have the patience to dedicate themselves to learning.]

The first written testimony we have regarding sins in the Christian tradition seems to me to be the most perceptive of all—assuredly a reflection of the subtlety of the desert fathers and of their participation in a living tradition. Among the hermits (who constituted the core of

---

[1] First Epistle to Maecenas (c. 20 B.C.).

Christianity in the first centuries), Evagrius (born in Greece) was the first to leave us writings. It is thought that he was the first to bring together in a coherent system the teaching of the desert fathers with respect to the life of prayer. Ascetic life for Evagrius is "the spiritual method whose aim is to purify that part of the soul that is the seat of passions."

It has been said that the desert fathers were able to elaborate the theory of sins because they also had the practice. Evagrius was heir to Origenes and to Gregory of Nyssa, as well as a direct disciple to one whom Dante, in his Paradise of the Contemplative, calls "Macarius the Great." Bamberger, in his introduction to *The Praktikos Chapters on Prayer*[2] says that Evagrius was the first "anatomist of the passions of the psyche, both in its manifestations in behavior as well as in its intra-psychic activity."

Citing Evagrius:

> Fear of God[3] fortifies your faith, my son. Continence, in turn, affirms this fear. Patience and hope make of this virtue something solid and implacable and give birth to *apatheia*. However, this *apatheia* gives rise to *ágape*, which guards the doorway to profound knowledge of creation. This knowledge is finally succeeded by theology (by which I mean, naturally, wisdom or *gnosis*) and supreme beatitude.

---

[2] Evagrius Ponticus, *The Praktikos Chapters on Prayer*, Cistercian Publications, Kalamazoo, Michigan, 1978.
[3] We should not conceive, tempting as it is to do so, the fear of God that the ancients talked of as the widespread neurotic fear of a celestial father, since it is clear that the ancient Jews acknowledged in the fear of God the fundament of supreme courage in the eyes of men (Such as in the example of the heroic prophet, Elias).

It is interesting to note that in the formulation of capital sins in Evagrius—the very first—the list comprises not seven, but rather eight. Of equal or greater interest is the fact that Evagrius does not call them sins, but rather deals with them as "thoughts"—"bad thoughts" (today we would say "destructive thoughts") and later on as "passionate thoughts."

Evagrius' list includes, apart from pride (which heads the current Gregorian list, but was the last in his), vainglory. He describes it as a subtle sin that is easily developed in souls who practice virtue, and that it leads them to want their efforts to be publicly known, since they seek acknowledgement. In addition to the seven sins that our Gregorian system recognizes, Evagrius recognizes the fault by which the devil is sometimes recognized when he is called "the lord of lies." Even before Evagrius, in the *Testament of the Patriarchs*, the "lying spirit" is spoken of and it appears that Evagrius inherited a more ancient tradition that recognizes the "lying spirit" as something underlying the other seven. An expert in human characters might perhaps nowadays find the expressions "falseness" or "inauthenticity" more appropriate. This is why, strictly speaking, one should not think of a different doctrine when subsequent theologists talked of the seven capital sins. It may be said that the recognition of this heptad, of this spectrum or of this rainbow of sin is common to the preceding and subsequent epochs.

For someone with practical, living knowledge of the psychology of sins, it will be easy to recognize that the *tristizia* (sadness) of Evagrius has been replaced by envy: envy is associated with sadness, since a feeling of a lack of value cannot avoid being a sad feeling, in the same way as the false abundance of pride makes this a cheerful passion. Evagrius' authority is of particular relevance in the description of *acidia* (indolence), which he called the "midday devil", and whose action in the inner life of the ascetic (i.e. one who seeks *hesichias, apatheia* or spiritual peace) is that lack of care (*chedia* in Greek) in which there is such a need for encouragement—since the temptation is great for one's concentration on the divine to be distracted and even for one to leave the cell itself. Evagrius tells us that indolence is the greatest of afflictions, and thus the occasion for the greatest purification.

It would appear that the desert fathers truly knew what forgetting God was (the curse of spiritual sloth) while monastics of subsequent generations—undoubtedly more extrovert and more active—gave the term a simple meaning of "sloth."[4] This shift in emphasis involved also the forgetting of the original meaning of *acidia*, which reflects a deterioration in the tradition. As has been the case so many times in the history of Christianity, a fanatical orthodoxy ended up being cut off from its sources and losing first hand knowledge. When originism was considered heresy, Evagrius himself became a heretic, and this certainly contributed to his being silenced and relatively forgotten—although this did not mean that he stopped being a most important link in the tradition.

Although it appears that the living understanding of capital sins had become lost in the heart of Christianity, we have seen a revival of interest in moods and the study of moods as fundamental as envy and pride in the world of psychology.

I mention envy first, since Melanie Klein is remembered more today than Karen Horney, who left us her

---

[4] *Acidia* entails spiritual sloth and not necessarily sloth with respect to action.

vision of neurosis as a selling of the soul to the devil in exchange for glory. Although for Horney, pride and the "tyranny of should" appeared to be fundamental in all neuroses (sustained by the need to maintain the idealized image that pride demands and sustains), I do not believe that Melanie Klein has explicitly left us a doctrine of envy as a fundamental psychopathology. However, it seems to me that she does do so with her view of envy as a sort of original sin: an ill that reaches us genetically, as an aspect of a death instinct inseparable from our nature.

After many years' experience as a psychotherapist, it seems to me that to interpret neurotic behavior from the viewpoint of envy or to interpret it as an expression of a fundamental impulse of pride is useful, and especially useful for people in whom one or the other constitutes the dominant sin or passion. It is natural since envious people (and by the way, I acknowledge these or them to be some of the most common characters in the world of psychotherapy) may see themselves much better in the light of an interpretation that reflects their envy at each step rather than in the light of an interpretation from the viewpoint of fear.

I say of fear and not something else, because fear has been the most common interpretation in psychology since Freud: it may be said that anxiety (irrational fear) is to the theory of Freud what the lying spirit is to that of Evagrius, namely a fundamental ill, the root of the unhealthy consciousness.

A colleague of mine in the psychiatric clinic at the University of Chile reproached psychoanalysts for using anxiety to explain everything. And I believe rightly so, since anxiety is used (and in second place, hate) to explain the acts of a person more often than pride, envy, and other specific forms of motivation deficiency. Since this interpretation is frequently the correct one, it fosters the temptation to overgeneralize.

The fundamental explanation of neurosis in psychoanalysis is thus childhood fear, which arises from the defenselessness and dependence of the child in the face of his or her parents' authority. This is the fear that has inhibited us, counteracting the force of our instinctiveness. Freud titled one of his books *Inhibitions, Symptoms and Anxiety*, with which he announced the idea that anxiety incites the inhibition from which symptoms arise (nowadays, we would prefer to say "neurotic suffering").

It is curious that Christianity, which has so extolled the blood of the martyrs, has not included cowardice among its sins. Or rather, it is not so curious. Nietzsche, in his *Genealogy of Morals*, left us the theory that our *ethos* is derived both from the Jewish people, who escaped slavery only to return to it again with their exile, and from early, persecuted Christianity. Nietzsche reproaches Christianity for what he called "the moral of slaves," the moral of castrated men—we would say in these post-Freudian times of ours—that has become concentrated in the virtue of humility, neglecting the acknowledgement of the old *arete* of the pagans. (The Greek term *arete* translates as virtue, but has the connotation of courage.)

It seems coherent to me that the recognition of fear as the fundamental individual problem has coincided with an epoch of great revolutions through which the world has been freed from a large dose of authoritarianism. It is logical to think that an authoritarian society, whose fundamental structure is one of imposing itself via fear, bases itself on secrecy. That is exactly why the recognition of the inner enemy has been therapeutic, as in some fairy tales where the enemy characteristically disappears when the hero pronounces his name.

Anyone who has surveyed all the terrain I have cited with respect to sins will surely be interested in a psychological theory that encapsulates all this while at the same time surpassing it, such as the theory that has inspired this book.

I refer to the application to the personality field of the "enneagram"—an emblematic expression of universal processes that has come down to us from a spiritual tradition preserved in Central Asia. It was through Gurdjieff that news publicly reached us for the first time of this esoteric Christianity with Babylonian, pre-Christian roots (an influence transmitted through Iranian spirituality) and which he characterized as a "fourth way" among the forms of classical spirituality.

The enneagram is a symbolic geometric construction characterized as emblematic of this tradition—and is the equivalent of an abstract expression of universal laws: the "law of three" and the "law of seven."* Without going into this in depth, I shall only say that, applied to human characters, the chart suggests that behind their multitude (nine in this view), there are three aspects of the psyche from which all the rest derive. And, moreover, one of these is the fundamental one: we shall conceive of it as an active unconscious.

Naturally, this has been rediscovered in psychology—and the unconscious is the fundamental idea of Freud, for whom the psychology of neurosis is the psychology of the unconscious. It would be more appropriate to stress the verb than the noun, however, and say "unconsciousness," the will to not know. Nowadays, the fundamental role of self awareness in the path of transformation has been recognized—at all

*Editor's note: For an introduction to these ideas, see works of G.I. Gurdjieff and P.D. Ouspensky, especially *In Search of the Miraculous*, by Ouspensky.

levels, from the body level, through behavior (particularly interpersonal behavior), to the emotional level, to thought and even to the awareness of awareness itself, which underlies spiritual traditions.

I do not know how many of my readers know the ideas of Gurdjieff through the testimony that Ouspensky has left us of his conversations, ideas, and activities. When I asked the people who came to me in California (where I was active in the 1970's) where they were coming from spiritually-speaking—what had been their sources, what things stood out in their spiritual autobiography—Gurdjieff was mentioned by at least half of them. Although until a short time ago his name was little known in the world, he was especially present for many seekers with a good sense of "smell," or as he would say, "with a well developed magnetic center."

Gurdjieff was a type of early 20th Century Russian Socrates. In my life, it was decisive for me as an adolescent to encounter a true spiritual teacher who made me realize that there were people who *knew*, in the fullest sense of the word. That living esoteric knowledge truly existed. At a later period of my life, I was part of the Gurdjieff school, or more precisely, of the school that remained after his death, when the center was established by Madame de Salzmann. I had the privilege to participate in a gathering of select disciples and experienced teachers during a meeting like none that had taken place since the beginning of the Second World War, when the center in Fontainebleau was sold and the already dispersed community came to hear Gurdjieff in the cafés of Paris. But precisely as a result of that privileged occasion of proximity to the heart of this school did I soon become disillusioned—in the sense that I did not seem to find a living lineage (in the fullest sense) in

31

the school that Gurdjieff had left behind. Consequently, and also so as not to lose hope of finding someone who embodied this knowledge of which Gurdjieff had brought us flashes, I became interested in Idries Shah when, in his book *The Sufis,* he gave us news of contact with this tradition that he calls Sufi but which the orthodox do not consider a typical expression of Sufism.

Through the information afforded by Shah, I learned of the *shattari* technique or rapid method, and of its survival among some Naqshbandi contemporaries. Through the materials made known to a study group run by Idries Shah to which I belonged, I also had news of the Sarmouni, of which no one had known anything since Gurdjieff's autobiography. I feel this information was a gift for me in so far as it led me to establish contact with someone who was to have a profound impact on my life.

The knowledge of protoanalysis and the spiritual disciplines related to the enneagram were less important for me than the living impact of the work carried out alongside Oscar Ichazo, who became known in South America in the 1960's as someone who had received his higher spiritual education in that remote school, with which he was not the only one who was seeking a connection.

In one of my early meetings with Ichazo, he described to me the disciplines I would pass through working with him. After "protoanalysis" (a period of becoming aware of one's own personality) would follow the work on virtues, through specialized techniques, as well as a temporary group task of "ego reduction" via one's own behavior and the criticism of others. This would prepare us for the work experience with the "catalysts" corresponding to the personal fixation—work that, if it were done well, must take one to a first level of mystical experience. His work would also include the development of the "centers," the activation of the chakras, the elevation of *kundalini,* and the sensitization of the *lataif.*

Despite the numerous doubts that contact with Ichazo inspired in me, I decided to accept his suggestion to afford myself the opportunity of the experience—and in simple words, I will say that I am happy to have done so. After the experience of an initial period of daily contact in Santiago de Chile came that of several months contact in the company of a group during the following year at the oasis of Azapa (near to Arica, in the far north of Chile)—a pilgrimage that was for me the beginning of a higher life.

Regarding that experience, the knowledge of proto-analysis and other applications of the enneagram to the comprehension of personality and inner work were something like a "farewell gift." Maybe this way of explaining it arises from within me because the gift of the desert was followed by the gift of beginning to understand (on my return to the world) things that have allowed me the satisfaction of helping others a great deal.

In the following pages, I propose to transmit succinctly what Ichazo transmitted with respect to the use of the enneagram as a map of the lower emotional center—or the domain of passions. Initially, however, I wish to mention that during one of the first meetings I had with Ichazo, he drew an enneagram with the names of the passions at the corresponding points and asked me to situate myself on the map. I suggested two hypotheses, and got it wrong both times.

At that time, I had years of psychoanalysis behind me, together with work along Gurdjieffian lines, Gestalt therapy, encounter groups, and other investigations. In spite of all this having helped me a great deal, I was unable to get it right, neither the first nor the second time. However, what he showed me (maybe the last thing that would have occurred to me) became obvious to me some hours later, and in the course of time contributed to a much deeper understanding of myself.

Ichazo said, as Gurdjieff before him, that it is difficult for people to know their own fundamental defects. And just as self-diagnosis is difficult, so is diagnosis of another. Ichazo, however, was a specialist and his legacy in this matter was to point out the dominant passion in each one of us who worked with him. The map he used as a guide in this was a specific application of the enneagram of personality: the enneagram of passions.

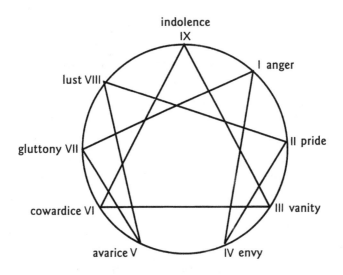

The Enneagram of Passions

The view of the "anatomy of neurosis" that the enneagram presents us demonstrates that the fear of the Freudians and the "lie" of the ancient rabbis are equally highlighted in importance; anxious inhibition and falsification of self, inauthenticity or vanity.

This view is highly consistent with what is implicitly present in the minds of modern psychotherapists—who have received the inheritance of Freudian and Humanistic psychology. Freud's theory of neurosis essentially has anxiety as its core concept, so that behavior may be defined as neurotic when it signifies an expression of something motivated by anxiety. The existentialist current in psychotherapy, on the other hand, is based on its vision of neurosis as a loss of authenticity. These two viewpoints are difficult to separate, however, since there would be no motivation for covering up if there were no wish to flee from anxiety via this mechanism, and it is difficult for fear not to be accompanied by treason against oneself, i.e. a loss of authenticity. This relationship is acknowledged in the representation of fear and falseness as symmetrical points that are joined by a line on the enneagram.

But these two pillars of neurosis—fear and inauthenticity—are understood according to the enneagram as components of a triad. A third cornerstone in the building of neurosis—as we have already seen—is inner laziness, a cognitive inertia, indolence. To call it, following Gurdjieff, "the devil of self-calming" has the virtue of making the person responsible for his or her unconscious.

Laziness of consciousness may be expressed either as spiritual sloth or more broadly as psychological sloth: a not wanting to know what is happening, not wanting to realize. It is expressed as a chronic self-distraction from oneself, accompanied at the same time by paying exaggerated attention to the outside world. An indolent position with respect to life is that of a heavy or excessively inert, over-stable psyche; its loss of subtlety and spontaneity culminates in robotization. On the behavioral plane, this lack of inwardness results in excessive inertia, phlegm, or passivity; at the most intimate level, alongside the forgetting of self, a loss of life.

The situation of indolence as a vertex of the central triangle of the enneagram of passions graphically indicates its relationship to the other two vertices of the triangle. The arrows on the chart mean that this loss of being and this disconnection of the person from him or herself is a result of covering up, and that in turn, the loss of being constitutes the dynamic core of fear: when life demands action, the lack of anchorage in the experience of the being itself makes us excessively vulnerable. We might say that in all fears there is fear of a future annihilation that is like a reverberation of an intuition of not being. In other words: in so far as indolence is an experience of the being that forgets itself, that is not seeking, but rather has a complacent, resigned attitude, fear is at the edge of not being, and tensely affirms itself in the face of intuited nothingness. On the other hand, as Goya says, the dream of reason creates monsters: the unconscious is the root of the fantasies that people create in the atmosphere of fear.

These are, therefore, the three cornerstones of the structure of the ego or personality: fear, vanity, and indolence or inertia of consciousness, presented as a loss of inwardness. The vicious circle of the three constitutes a dynamic theory of neurosis. "Dynamic" because each of these entities constitutes an energy focus from which a certain type of action proceeds, as well as because the tripartite theory includes the metadynamic view: a dynamic of reciprocal transformation among the three basic neurotic motivations.

I hope that others find this view of neurosis as inspiring as I do; it implies a "therapeutic" view in the broad sense of a conception of the process of liberation: it is a process of becoming aware, that is accompanied by an unmasking of oneself before others, by an overcoming of inhibitions and a relative transcendence of fear. More generally, a psychotherapist who gets to know the enneagram will inescapably contemplate the therapeutic process as one of going against the stream of the nine passions we shall review in this chapter.

Before expounding the circle of fundamental faults or sins, however, I should say that the circular representation implies that no single one stands out. Having said so, I shall start the review of the six not included in the central triad with the one that is situated at point one on the enneagram: anger, whose proximity to indolence of consciousness acknowledges the old saying that "anger is blind." We shall see that the character that has anger as its motivational core is not a violent character, but rather, on the contrary, is someone who opposes violence both in him or herself and in others. The violence he or she blindly commits is not exactly what we call violence, but rather is expressed in a critical attitude, an interest in power, in being demanding and dominating.

The saying that anger is blind is not concretely expressed as the violence of an Ajax who thrashes out in the dark against bulls: it may express itself as subtly as in the situation characterized by Quino in a cartoon that represents a shepherd with a harsh, serious expression who in his implicit criticism of the stupidity of one among his sheep (which does not eat randomly) fails to see that it has sketched a smiling shepherd image on the meadow; and he would be even less capable of conceiving that it wished to communicate something to him in such a friendly and intelligent way.

For a person in whom anger constitutes a dominant passion but who is not visibly irate, manifest violence is the characteristic expression of lust. When this character predominates, the psychological attitude is not to negate or control agression, but on the contrary to overvalue it. Whereas anger is a rigid hand that controls, lust involves a defiant negative to repressive control.

Although lust is conventionally identified with sexual passion, we understand it here in an inner sense, as an excessive desire for more: a passion of intensity. Naturally, sex satisfies this intensity; but a lustful person squanders his or her energy and seeks intensity in everything, both in the world of sensory stimuli and in that of action.

Lust appears to be a completely opposite attitude to indolence. While indolence is expressed as phlegm, as the tendency towards immutability and lack of passion, lust appears to involve an excess of passion. The lustful person who introspectively considers his or her lust, however, may discover that precisely because he or she does not feel, he or she needs to feel so much; precisely as a consequence of a process of desensitization, he or she desperately wants to replace this lack of sensitivity with intensity.

We have said something about the three passions that are represented in the upper part of the enneagram and which we may call the family of indolence. Let us now go on to consider one that is situated at the opposite pole of the enneagram, integrated in the family of fear. Why does avarice hang on to its objects other than out of fear? Naturally, we are not talking here solely about avarice for money, but rather of a broader retentive expression of the psyche, which is like a defense against imaginary privation. Avarice is also something like being paralyzed with fear, and goes hand in hand with making economies in living—not investing in acts (and in particular, in relationships), reserving oneself for a possible better future.

But not-giving, typical of avarice, implies not only underlying fear, but also an aspect of shortcoming that links avarice with envy. Envy may be described as an intense desire to incorporate something on the basis of a vivid sentiment of shortcoming. In psychoanalytical terms, envy is called a "cannibalistic," devouring passion.

Envy, at the same time, is halfway between avarice and vanity, belonging (together with pride, and in a symmetric position with respect to it) to the family of vanity. If envy longs to be filled, pride already feels full, and offers to fill others. Envy asks, it desires from its feeling of shortcoming; pride offers, gives, from a basic feeling of abundance.

There is no doubt that this expression of envy causes much more pain than that of pride, which in itself is a pleasurable expression. As it is the essence itself of pride to have a good, grand image of oneself, it is difficult for this to be felt to be a problem; hence the pedagogical wisdom of the ancient spiritual masters who wished especially to point out the gravity of pride, naming it the foremost of sins. This is how we encounter it, for example, in Dante's *Purgatory*.

The logic of each point in the enneagram representing the result of interaction of the neighboring points is also expressed in pride. Pride shares with vanity falsification and emphasis on one's own image, and it shares with anger, since pride adopts, as does the angry person, an expression of self-assertiveness and superiority.

Finally, there is gluttony, which the enneagram indicates as being a neighbor to fear, even though the greedy character is not a person who consciously tends to feel intimidated. The glutton who examines him or herself in depth, however, gets to understand that his or her search for pleasure as well as his or her avoidance of pain are escape reactions to anxiety, and a form of running away from oneself. Naturally, we are not talking here only about gluttony for food. The gluttony described by theologists corresponds to what psychoanalysis calls "oral-receptive," which constitutes a psychic expression similar to that of a breast-feeding child, and which may also be considered as a regression of the adult to this more privileged childhood position in life.

Gluttony not only entails hedonism in a sensual sense, but also in a broader sense not wanting to be uncomfortable and the particular pleasure of non-frustration—i.e. self-indulgence. The theologists were also right in placing gluttony at the beginning of the most ancient series of sins (before being replaced by pride): since the gluttonous attitude leads to more pleasure than other attitudes and is therefore particularly tempting. The obstacle that gluttony can mean in the path of maturing may be understood in the light of the amusing aphorism of Oscar Wilde's, who said, "I can resist everything except temptation."

Although gluttony belongs to the family of fear, its link to lust is equally close. This is revealed by the fact that those who are predominantly gluttonous are similar to the lustful both in terms of hedonism and rebelliousness. Where lust seeks intensity, greed seeks pleasure (and perhaps even more decisively, non pain).

It seems to me that the circle of the nine basic passions presented by Ichazo constitutes a refinement on the octad of Evagrius, not only because of the inclusion of fear among the sins, but rather due to its constituting precisely a circle and not only an ennead: an ordering of the passions, a "psychodynamic" model. That is to say, a model that gives a notion of the origin of each of the passions as a result of a kind of hybridizing of its neighbors, the whole set arising from a basic triad, each of these basic passions constituting a transformation of another.

Clearly, the idea that some sins proceed from others is not new in Christian literature: in particular, Casianus, who after spending twenty years in Egypt came to live in Marseilles, already spoke of this in the 5th century. Each of the eight of the last books of his Institute is dedicated to one of the sins, and is illustrated with biblical examples and anecdotes from the Egyptian monks. According to Casianus, each of the sins derives from the preceding one, according to an order that commences with gluttony and ends with pride.

But it seems to me that the ordering of the passions in the enneagram goes further than the notions of Casianus, both in exactitude and in detail. Apart from the psychodynamic links between fear, falseness, and indolent laziness, they indicate the unidirectional paths between the points of the enneagram—psychodynamic links between the other passions—pointing to the following: how anger, when it turns on itself, becomes self-destructive envy; how envious voracity, seen in the mirror, becomes generosity fed by pride; how the attitude of seductive conquest of pride becomes the domineering conquest of lust; how lustful greed, via self-negation becomes the impotent greed of avarice; how making economies and depriving oneself of avarice engenders, as compensation, the attitude of self-wasting and self-indulgence of gluttony; and how once again sweet self-indulgence engenders an opposite: the austere severity of anger.

More significantly, however, the transpersonal psychology expounded by Ichazo constitutes the expression of a living tradition of experiential knowledge that was transmitted in an experiential manner. A notable aspect of this is the living comprehension that he has brought us of those characters in which one or another of the passions predominates. (The courses on this characterology that have become part of the training program of the Jesuits in the USA and in the English-speaking countries testify of this.)

Clearly the fathers of the Church not only considered the set of sins as a common impurity, but also recognized human types according to whether one or another sin was dominant. This view is reflected in Dante's presentation of sins in particular incarnations, in which he exhibits his particular genius for character portrayal. In his treatise on the "Dark Night of the Soul," St. John of the Cross also depicts characters when dealing with the forms that each of the sins assumes during this period of trials that follow mystic awakening and which precede spiritual maturity.

We find psychological errors in Dante, however, when we become familiar with the psychology of enneatypes that provides the theoretical grounding of Ichazo's "protoanalysis." Ichazo imparted a personal insight akin to that of a therapist rather than that of the traditionally-trained priest.

One of the notable contributions of Ichazo's way of implementing protoanalysis lies in his accurate diagnoses—as already hinted in the anecdote I have related. As I said, self-diagnosis is difficult. Or, at least, difficult when starting from the simple question of whether it is pride that predominates in one's own life, or envy, fear, or some other "deficient motivation."

However, the task is somewhat less difficult when

one has more information than that Ichazo provides. In particular, it is less difficult to be wrong in questions of behavior than in questions of emotional or motivational states, such as when one asks oneself whether one is gluttonous or lustful. Recognition of our less commendable motivations and the evaluation of their importance in our relations with others may be flawed, but we cannot ignore the reality of our behavior.

It is in terms of behavior that scientific descriptions of psychological aberrations are typically expressed, and the different syndromes of psychiatry and psychology are no more than the exaggerated expression of a series of personality styles that are centered on one or other of the passions.

It was natural that as a psychotherapist I gradually realized from the beginnings of my work with Ichazo that each of the sins or passions corresponds to a certain character pathology among those recognized in medicine and psychology. Through subsequent practice, I was able to appreciate with growing clarity how the possibility of recognizing one's own prototype among the characters becomes easier when one is familiar not only with the enneagram of passions, but also with the enneagram of pathologies.

Although character pathologies are no more than the most problematic manifestations of character traits that are considered normal, it is also true that what is "normal" is simply "ill" (or if we prefer religious terminology, "sinful") to a lesser degree. Thus the knowledge of pathologies is of particular interest in making our "shadow" more visible through its exaggeration. (Also collectively, we have little by little come to understand what is called "health" through the study of what is pathological.)

Although I shall talk in detail in the following chapter about the nine characters constituted around each of the fundamental passions, I shall set out here in a complementary way to the enneagram of passions or sins, the corresponding sequence of aberrations of personality according to the enneagram, in the hope that like the exaggerated images that we see reflected in a trick mirror, this will help the "normal" reader to become aware of his or her subtle pathologies.

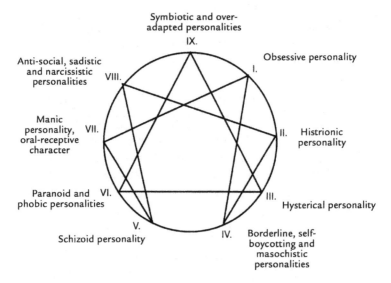

The Enneagram of Pathologies[5]

In this new enneagram, I have written "obsessive personality" at point one. This means that the character extreme corresponding to anger is the one called since the 19th Century "obsessive personality" (or more pre-

---

[5] As can be seen, I have preferred not to homogenize the characteristic vocabulary of different authors, conserving the terms "personality," "character," etc., in accordance with the use of each.

cisely nowadays "obsessive personality disorder"). That is according to the nomenclature of the *Diagnostic and Statistical Manual of Mental Illnesses* elaborated by the North American Medical Association or DSM-III as it has become universally known.

This is a rigid, perfectionist, and excessively controlled character in which there exists a great desire for order and excessive seriousness.

These are personalities who are excessively worried about details, the rules to follow, and punctuality—to such a degree that this interferes with the relevance of their activity and with the completion of the tasks they undertake. They exhibit an excessively scrupulous and moralistic tendency, which seems to strangle the spirit of these people, as well as their capacity to make friends and the spontaneous expression of their emotions.

I have situated the character called histrionic in the DSM-III at the second point in the enneagram, which corresponds to pride. This term has recently come to replace the old word "hysterical," in which too many variances of meaning overlapped. Paraphrasing the synthesis of this personality offered by Lorna S. Benjamin[6]: "the person seeks to be the center of attention and deeply desires the love and care of a powerful person who can at the same time be controlled through charm. The basic position is one of friendly trust accompanied by a disrespectful hidden agenda according to which the goal is to obtain love at any cost."

The vanity-centered character corresponds to the one that used to be called "hysterical" and whose formulation the authors of the DSM-III mistakenly considered to be an imperfect approximation of "histrionic." This is a similar character to the histrionic in being characteristically "plas-

---

[6] Lorna Smith Benjamin, *Interpersonal Diagnosis and Treatment of Personality Disorders*, The Guilford Press, New York, 1993.

45

tic" (i.e. as a result of the capacity to intentionally adopt different roles), but whose description is not to be found in the DSM-III—perhaps due to its being a cheerful, efficient character that does not appear to be pathological and coincides with the North American style. Its most distinctive characteristic is not to be found in the description of hysterical personality, but rather in the observation of Erich Fromm relative to what he proposed to call the "marketing orientation of personality."

"One must be fashionable in the personality market, and to be fashionable one must know what kind of personality is the most highly valued. This knowledge is transmitted in a general way through the entire process of education, from kindergarten to university, and is implemented by the family. The knowledge acquired at an early age is, however, not sufficient: it stresses only certain general qualities such as adaptability, ambition and sensitivity in relation to the changing expectation of others. The more specific image of success models is obtained through other sources. Illustrated magazines, newspapers and newsreels show images and life histories of successful people in many varieties." [7]

More than one characterological syndrome corresponding to the expression of envy is to be found nowadays in the DSM-III. One of the most typically impulsive and dramatically self-destructive forms is what is called the "borderline" personality. Lorna S. Benjamin describes it as one in which there is an unhealthy fear of abandonment and an exaggerated need for protection and help, as well as a desire for physical proximity to those who provide this. The basic position of friendly dependence becomes hostile control if the protector or

[7]Erich Fromm. *Man for Himself: An Inquiry into the Psychology of Ethics* Holt, Rhinehart and Winston, New York 1964.

lover does not give enough (and what is given is never enough). The person does not allow him or herself to be cheerful or successful, in an implicit attachment to his or her condition of need and frustration.

Another category still under study is what might be translated as the "self-boycotting personality," which corresponds to the better-known concept of "masochistic character" (though not to what Lowen, and by extension Bioenergetics, calls the masochistic character). Horney has written extensively about the mechanism of complaining and demanding through suffering that characterizes these people, as well as of their affective dependence and their self-belittlement.

The characterological syndrome that corresponds to avarice is what is known today as the "schizoid" personality. This is characterized by indifference towards human relations, lack of communication, lack of expressivity, the limiting of one's own desires, and social clumsiness.

More than one characterological syndrome corresponds to the expression of fear. One of these is a timid, hesitant character, which in the DSM-III appears through two different descriptions: the "dependent" personality and the "avoidant" personality. I am convinced that these two personalities are not fundamentally different, but are varieties of a single syndrome in which the fearful need for support and timidity with respect to approaching others coexist.

The basic personality is one of excessive submission towards a dominant personality, which is expected to play a protective, guiding parental role. The desire to maintain this link is such that it can lead to the person even allowing abuse. As he or she considers him or herself incompetent, he or she cannot live without the support of the person to whom he or she is subordinate.

On the other hand, psychoanalytical literature reveals a counterphobic personality which finds its closest echo in the paranoid personality of the DSM-III (except that the description made of the latter corresponds to the most aberrant cases). This form of personality is one in which fear is negated in response to an implicit fear of fear, as well as an exaggerated implicit defense strategy that acts via attacking.

This is a personality that tends to interpret the behavior of others as intentionally antagonistic or as having evil intent, distrusting their friendship or reliability. He or she perceives threatening significations where there are none, becomes furious at imaginary insults, suffers and tortures due to jealousy, and is excessively willing to attack.

Finally, there is a form of expression of fear that might be called a "Prussian personality," which in diagnostic practice nowadays is confused with the obsessive personality: these are people that are afraid of making mistakes who find refuge in an excessive adherence to rational or ideological canons and in the cultivation of order and precision. They are afraid of being accused of imperfection, and their search for order leads them to a position of control that is inconsiderate towards others. There is excessive discipline, emotional control, and self-criticism, apart from criticism towards others.

The personality corresponding to gluttony was first described by Karl Abraham, a disciple of Freud's, who proposed for this personality a designation of "oral-optimistic" or "oral-receptive" personality. In the current diagnostic code, the closest description is the "narcissistic" personality, characterized by a great need for affection, support, admiring deference, and the expectation of special treatment in virtue of the person's talents or merits.

Although the character corresponding to lust closely corresponds to the description that Wilhelm Reich gave to the "phallic-narcissistic" personality, in current-day nomenclature the extreme form of this human type is labeled "anti-social personality," and in its most exaggerated form, "sadistic personality." Perhaps the best description is the one proposed by Karen Horney of a "vindictive" personality: one in which the individual represses his or her caring, weak side and aims to compensate an infantile sentiment of impotence with respect to the environment through a search for power and an illusion of invulnerability.

This character has an excessive desire to control others, at the same time as a great need for independence and a great resistance to control by others—who tend to be looked down upon. Aggression and intimidation are placed at the service of independence and domination. The anti-social person generally presents him or herself as a friendly, social person, but deep down he or she does not care what happens to others or even to him or herself; therein lies his or her capacity to take risks.

The indolent character was vividly described by Ernst Kretschmer as a "hypomanic" variant of the "cyclothymic" personality. It also corresponds to the "masochistic" personality of Bioenergetics, but does not find a clear echo in the North American Diagnostic Manual. This is easy to understand, as failure to adapt tends to be considered more pathological than over-adaptation and this type of personality is one with problems of not acknowledging problems and an excessive adaptation to the social environment.

The clinical characterology of today highlights behavior more than the dynamic or motivational aspect, and I am convinced that the motivational characterology that the enneagram of passions reflects constitutes, in so far as it is a dynamic mapping, a decisive complement for those who seek information with the aim of broadening their awareness. The therapeutic value of the *insight* into the emotional core of neurosis can only be compared to the therapeutic power of the *insight* into this cognitive core of neurosis that the "protoanalysis" presented by Ichazo declares to be the most fundamental and resistant to change. I shall talk about this implicitly as part of the more in-depth treatment of the nine basic characters in the following chapter.

II

The Circle of the
Nine Basic Characters

To speak of "characters" or human types is somewhat
different from speaking about "pathologies" or "personality disorders," since the abnormal symptoms described
by psychologists and psychiatrists correspond only to
the most pronounced manifestation of certain human
types. While for example, according to a recent book
only around three percent of the patients that turn to
therapists for help in the United States are diagnosed as
schizoid, I am sure that the type of character distinguished by traits that, when extreme, the medical profes-
sion calls schizoid is to be found at a considerably higher
proportion.

However, it is highly relevant to talk about
pathologies, since in a certain way the distinction
between what is sane and what is pathological is more
conventional than real. In other words: more apparent

than profound and more quantitative than qualitative. Although within each personality type people with different levels of pathology *versus* integration—from psychosis, passing through neurosis, to the diverse grades of evolution towards sainthood (a condition of ego transcendence)—can be identified, it is also clear that the style of personality of the "sane" or "normal" constitutes the residue of a pathology. Considered in depth, the difference between healthy and ill people is not so much the difference between the presence or absence of neurotic motivations (i.e. sins), but rather the difference in how much more than this there is in the person, or to what degree the person has managed to be the master of his or her own house instead of the slave of his or her conditioning. Thus, even in cases of advanced self-realization, we can see that the person exhibits residues of his or her childhood conditioning—only the character traits have become useful rather than constituting impediments.

Nowadays, when the books on the enneagrams of personality are awakening growing interest in the public, there are those who criticize an orientation that insists too much on what is pathological—and it seems to me that this protest generally reflects a resistance to self-questioning and a preference for a pleasant and innocuous, *light* way of getting information that is so typical of our age, which has rebelled against the traditional insistence of Christian culture on sin. For this reason, I will make no effort to please those who may have wanted a presentation of characters in the habitual style of astrology books, which mention favorable or unfavorable aspects for each planet or constellation.

Personality, in so far as it is a residue of our childhood strategies (to obtain a love that did not reach us naturally in a world of lack), is an important form of conditioning. Clearly, the attention to appearances of the vain may be a trait that makes them desirable as interior decorators, and the tolerance of routine of the indolent, trustworthy administrators. However, the value of these behaviors for the individual is much less than the value of recognizing their limiting and conditioned nature and how they are part of a parasitic aspect of the personality, which will have less power over one's life if it is better known. As Gurdjieff said, when a machine knows itself, it becomes responsible for its acts and can no longer be called a machine.

In the previous chapter, we started to talk about the enneagram of the passions as a set of inner states that coexist in the mind of each individual, but we ended up employing the enneagram as an organizing map for the set of pathologies recognized by the scientific world. We shall continue in this chapter to employ the enneagram as a way of organizing the territory of human types—which has an obvious advantage over their simple enumeration, because such an organization of characterology indicates relationships between each point and the neighboring points in the circle, as well as the points that are connected to it according to the inner lines. Although it is not my aim to go into this in detail[1] here, I shall draw attention to some of these relationships, starting with the fact that the nine characters are organized into three groups of three, in accordance with the areas that surround each of the "corners" on the chart.

[1] I have developed this theme in my book *Character and Neurosis: An Integrative View*, Gateways/IDHHB, Inc., 1994.

Symmetry and Polarity in the Enneagram

When we think not of the individual, but rather of human types, what is noticeable is the air of family of the types that are to be found in the three corners of the enneagram: we may speak of a *hysteroid* group of characters, a *schizoid* group, and another that is *rigid* or *anti-intraceptive*. (I do not say anti-introverted because this does not constitute the opposite of social introversion, but rather the opposite of inwardness or interest in the contents of the mind, technically known as intraception.) What is characteristic of the three characters that are represented at the top of the enneagram (I, VIII and IX) is their interest in *not* looking towards the subtle world of life experiences; a non-inwardness that goes hand in hand with active extroversion. In contrast, the dramatic and *socially* extrovert characters (II, III and IV) are located in the area of the angle on the right, whereas the angle on the left entails an introverted disposition (V, VI and VII)—although in Enneatype VII (EVII), the underlying introversion is compensated by superficial sociability.

The symmetry between the left and right side of the enneagram is not only one of social introversion/extroversion: it also constitutes a polarity of rebellion/seduction. The right side is more social or socialized; the left, more antisocial. This is the same polarity that exists between hysterical and psychopathic, both studied by Eysenk.

There also exists a polarity between the upper and lower parts of the enneagram of characters. We may speak of a polarity of *tough-mindedness* and *tender-mindedness* in relation to the degree of intraception or inwardness. Characteristically, the lower region of the enneagram is that of the "poor of spirit"; i.e. of those who are in contact with their sense of lack at the heart of their being. At the opposite (upper) pole are to be found those who have turned a deafer ear to their inner hurting, and who therefore feel immensely more satisfied. In contrast, Enneatypes IV and V (in the lower region of the enneagram) are those who are fashionable in psychoanalysis: borderline and schizoid personalities. These are, one could say, the "borderline," the most problematic. Or more precisely, the problem-ridden, in contrast to the characters of points VIII, IX and I, whose secret problem is not having problems. The case of these characters that science considers so pathological serves to illustrate the theoretical formulation of equivalence among them. The "poor of spirit" (a term which in the original Aramaic would translate literally as "lepers") are those who seek more intensely—and those who seek a lot, find.

The enneagram of characters is thus organized in terms of a symmetry of social introversion versus extroversion and a polarity of intraception or inwardness and anti-intraception or rejection of inwardness.

But things are a little more complex by virtue of the different proportion to which the three possible pairs that make up the sides of the central triangle may combine. Thus, for instance, we find that the character we designate as Enneatype VII, though secretly introverted, is apparently hyper-extroverted or manic, and Enneatype I, blind to his or her ignorance, believes him or herself to be introverted.

I shall now explain in more detail the way in which each of the characters expresses in its behavior its dominant passion and its explicit error of perspective—which entails a cognitive aspect or an overvalued interpersonal strategy, a mistaken position with respect to the world of others and even with respect to themselves. To the description of each of the human types of Protoanalysis (Enneatypes) in terms of its main personality traits, I shall add a consideration of the characteristic way in which the person *defends* him or herself from becoming aware of the world, and I shall include quotations from the description of characters from the most ancient of the classics: Theophrastus, the successor of Aristotle, who considered the theme of sufficient interest to dedicate his attention to it at the age of one hundred.

As a complement to the erudition of Theophrastus, however, I shall fall back on popular humoristic observations: the old Italian caricatures that were part of the cultural movement called the *Commedia dell'Arte* and some contemporary caricatures that circulate in the form of jokes or cartoons and are testimony of an implicit, non-professional psychological subtlety.

Let us start off with pride, to do honor to the Gregorian and Dantean tradition.

ENNEATYPE II: PRIDE

The choice of pride in first place is undoubtedly in keeping with the thirst for attention and distinction of the proud character. Moreover, it seems to me to be a wise strategy of the ancient spiritual guides to underline the importance of this passion, which, like gluttony, expresses itself through an indulgent character that is less given than others to feel at fault. It is difficult for the proud to progress spiritually, however, without being helped to become aware, without having their evasion of displeasure and lack of self-criticism pointed out, since this lack of self-criticism means that the subject feels superior, great, worthy of deference, important. However, deep down they have a great need for love, and their entire life is oriented around this need to be loved through a falsification of reality. That is what the inflation of their self-image demands.

Although pride is a passion through which we see ourselves as superior to what we are, it is worth clarifying that this feeling of superiority is not commonly expressed as arrogance and may pass unnoticed by others. Those who "truly" have a good opinion of themselves irradiate their self-complacency in such a way that it is instantaneously shared by those surrounding them, without the need to make their quality explicit through performance or virtuous acts. They are so convinced of their merits that they do not feel they have to convince others, not even themselves; rather they revel in the result of this self-inflation: well being. While the majority of people suffer the distance that separates them from the ideal, proud people, mistaking themselves for their ideal, revel in themselves.

However, this is not a "virtuous" ideal, as in the case of the irascible character. Their virtue is not the virtue of discipline or one that lies in self-control, but is that supreme, though spontaneous, virtue that is the ability to love. Feeling him or herself to be replete with love, the proud person feels like a "grand" person, capable of giving to others and worthy of receiving the best from them.

And he or she is "truly" a loving person; it is only when taking the path of self-knowledge that he or she discovers how much this lovingness is basically a role that he or she mistakes for reality. One might say that deep down this person does not love others for themselves, but loves rather to feel capable of love and hence a complete person, worthy of being loved. But no matter how visible the seductive nature of their love is to others, it is difficult for them to see this themselves. Let us not forget that pride is situated in the Enneagram next to lying, simulation, falsification of self. To manage to understand that they have lived life taking the self-created movie of themselves as reality is particularly complicated since their loving, pleasant, and empathic behavior brings them so much positive feedback.

In contrast to other characters who are driven to question themselves as a result of the hardships of life, the proud character does not receive so many challenges compared to those who face the world from a position of more competitive superiority, like that of the neighboring points in the Enneagram.

The world knows the game of the proud well, as revealed by the expression *femme fatale* used to designate certain women who are highly attractive. It is implicitly understood that the attractiveness of the person is good for her, but not at all for those who "succumb" to her. Something similar is meant by "vamp."

A classical interpretation of this character is given to us by Emile Zola in *Nana*—the beautiful prostitute who ruins her noble, lost lover; another is *Carmen*, irresistible, vital, and provocative.

Although Theophrastus[2] does not include a character he calls proud[3] in his collection—he does include "braggart"[4]; according to him, this character's behavior tends

---

[2] The material on Theophrastus in the original Spanish version of this text was included in my book *Character and Neurosis*, and was translated into Spanish by Irma Pérez. The related notes belong to her.
[3] The arrogant person is a better example of the phallic narcissist (Enneatype VIII) than of the proud enneatype.
[4] According to the Spanish version of *Caracteres de Teofrasto* (Gredos, Madrid, 1988), bragging is described as the mania for grandiosity. (Translator's Note in Spanish edition).

towards a unique capacity for compulsive lying, a concept that psychiatry calls "fantastic pseudology," which has been associated with the histrionic personality disorder.

"Bragging seems to be a fictitious invention of non-existent qualities." Theophrastus begins by talking about this bragging as the grandiosity of the image that is presented to others and which goes beyond a mere exhibition of dignity. His lying becomes evident when he tells us that the braggart "is he who in the bazaar tells strangers about the great sums of money he has invested at sea, and informs them of what a great business this type of loan is, of his losses and profits. While boasting in this way, he sends his slave to the bank to deposit a ridiculous sum of money."

Although adulation in itself is an aspect of characters VII and III of the Enneagram, we find in Theophrastus's description rather the adulation that corresponds to the strict sense of the word; from which it is possible to identify it as an example of Enneatype II. (It is interesting to observe that in the majority of versions of Theophrastus's book, it is this image of the flatterer that occupies the first place.)

Citing his text:

The flatterer is an individual capable of saying to the person with whom he is taking a walk: "Have you noticed how people look at you? It happens to no one else in Athens apart from you. Yesterday in the Portico they sang your praises. There were more than thirty people sitting there and when the question of who the man of most worth is came up, everyone present started and finished with your own name." While he continues to say these pleasantries and the like, he takes a piece of lint from your gown, and if a blade of grass carried by the wind lands on your hair, he removes it while adding with a smile: "You see? As I haven't seen you for two days, your beard is full of gray hairs and yet for your age your hair is black like no other." No sooner does this person start to speak, but the flatterer makes everyone else be quiet, he praises him when he hears him and the moment the other person stops speaking, he exclaims: "Magnificent."

In this image, we can observe a subtle and implicit form of flattery that distinguishes itself from the simple affirmation of the worth of the other person. The pride of the other is indirectly satisfied via manifestations of esteem, concern, and admiration, and via the stimulation of the flattery of others. Theophrastus's description also calls one's attention to a certain generosity in the flatterer's behavior:

And it goes without saying that he is also capable, as if he were a slave, of doing the shopping in the women's market, without even stopping to catch his breath ... He asks his host if he is not cold and before he pronounces a word, wraps him warmly with his cloak.

In this last comment, it is insinuated that this supposedly generous concern may be invading and lacking in tact with respect to the desires of the other person—a trait that is discussed in greater depth in the case of characters like the "inopportune" character and the "meddler."[5] With respect to the latter, he affirms:

Meddling seems to be an excessively good disposition both with respect to words as well as acts. The meddler is an individual capable, after having stood up, of promising what he is not going to fulfill... He insists

[5] The "officious" person is the character of the "meddler" according to the Spanish version of *Caracteres de Teofrasto* cited above (translator's note in Spanish edition).

that the slaves mix more wine than the guests can drink ... He acts as a guide along a short cut and then cannot find the place he wanted to go to ... He likewise appears before a superior officer to ask when he is going to decide to begin the battle and what the password is going to be for the day after tomorrow ... At the tomb of a recently deceased woman, he has the name of her husband, her father, her mother, that of the deceased woman herself, and her date of birth inscribed. As if this were not enough, he also asks for it to be engraved that they were respectable people.

In this last image, Theophrastus gives us a caricature of the person who bothers others with his exaggerated, unnecessary, and intrusive way of showing esteem.

The proud character was caricatured in the *Commedia dell'Arte* in the "mask" of Colombina. Carla Poesio tells us in her book *Conoscere le maschere italiane*:[6]

Is Colombina the one who cleans the house? Or a damsel who has fun playing with dust? It is not so easy to answer. She is a chambermaid, yes, but elegant and refined like a princess. This beautiful girl handles the feather duster like a piece of precious porcelain. She walks with tiny steps as if dancing, and touches up her tiny coffietta and a curl in each mirror and in each windowpane. She thinks about everything except dusting the furniture and the paintings ... She is lively, full of spirit, likeable. She will certainly not be a great housekeeper, but in compensation she is clever and eloquent like other servants—like Arlecchino and Brighella in their own times. She is a girl who is never in the dumps, she not only uses her tongue to speak of the stars, of smiles and looks, and she also knows how to face up sassily to an overly severe master.

---

[6]Edizioni Primavera, Florence, 1982.

Colombina
Illustration by Giorgio Sansoni, © Edizioni Primavera, Florence

The defense mechanism in the histrionic character is what is called pure and simple "repression," though its full name is not so simple: "repression of the ideational representative of the instinct" according to Freud. In short, these are people who, despite the apparent freedom with which they feel and express their emotions, do not allow themselves to *know* what they feel. Of course, we may say that they do not *want* to assume responsibility for this, but the limits between bad faith and the unconscious are mysterious, as Sartre has so aptly remarked in his critique of Freud.

ENNEATYPE VII: GLUTTONY

In the glutton, the pleasure of eating is surely the least important of his or her manifestations, and may even be masked by an excessive dietary-spiritual concern, born of the fact that these characters feel unconsciously guilty over their gluttony and feel bad about it. (They seek to be excessively pure.) It seems to me that in today's world, there are more people of this character than of others among those who think that "we are what we eat" and favor the macrobiotic or vegetarian diets and more generally, natural medicine.

The passion for more and better that is gluttony manifests itself in a generalized form in interpersonal relations as a desire to be liked, to be popular, to receive admiration. Often, the gluttonous man adores his mother, and his life revolves—as in Fellini's film *8 1/2*—around an idealized image of woman, who represents the beginning and end of all pleasures and the good things in life. But intellectual gluttony is also important, making this the most curious type of character, both in the sense of a search for new horizons and experiences in the concrete world and in the abstract search in the world of ideas. This character feels attracted to the final frontiers of knowledge with all that mystery and the exotic entail.

Referring to an even more fundamental defect than gluttony, Ichazo characterized this type of personality as the "charlatan." Certainly these characters are loquacious, and their loquacity serves both to exhibit special knowledge as well as to "entangle" others in their ideas, projects, and desires. Their loquacity mainly serves their gluttony—that is, it entails a way of obtaining the object of their desires through good explanations. And these good explanations are particularly important when the question is to go beyond the limits that the environment imposes.

These are "cheeky" characters that get what they want due to their likeableness and their ingenious arguments. But talkativeness stems not only from good reasons, but also principally from the capacity to enchant— which entails not only intelligence and astuteness, but also a certain level of well-being and happiness, without which these people could sustain neither their rise nor their capacity to give advice. To achieve this level of well-being, they naturally have to fool themselves—since the level of pain and conflicts is not intrinsically greater or lesser in one character than in another—and in this self-deception converge the need to maintain a charming façade and gluttony itself, since even more important than the desire to please is the avoidance of pain that this hedonism brings with it.

The gluttonous character is situated in the Enneagram halfway between cowardice and lust. It could be described as masked cowardice, in which the person finds refuge in pleasure in order to flee anxiety. It could at the same time be understood as a toned-down form of lust, in which more intensity is not sought at the cost of pain—as in EVIII—but rather more sweetness. This is not a "motorbike and rock'n'roll" type hedonism, but rather a hedonism of what is agreeable and the avoidance of what is disagreeable. The glutton shares rebelliousness with the lustful character, but this is not an open, direct form of rebelliousness, but indirect and subtle, for which a different word is more appropriate: anticonventionalism. This character disdains the habitual and always feels attracted to the unusual and innovation.

Maybe the most marked traits of the "narcissist" of North American psychiatry and of the DSM-III are the good image of oneself and feeling one has rights in virtue of a special talent, which certainly applies to EVII. Although these people project a good image of themselves and to a greater extent than other types feel well-being, we can say that this is the fruit of a continuous self-propaganda campaign with respect to the world and themselves that acts as a counterweight to a likewise conscious sense of insecurity. Perhaps this is why the good impression that they try hard to make on others is not motivated by an arrogant, megalomaniac, or extensively superior presentation of self, but rather corresponds to that of a friendly person who insists on an egalitarian approach, while expecting special recognition not only of his or her talent but also as a result of his or her modesty and fraternal disposition.

Very present in this character is the defense mechanism called "rationalization," which means attributing to one's own acts a different, more socially admirable or acceptable motivation than the real one—essentially the negation of the gluttonous, opportunistic part of the person, while making a conspicuous display of being generous and obliging. When describing a character of this type, Elias Canetti[7] observes, "they do not even allow you to offer them a cup of coffee."

An important trait of this character, not yet mentioned, is humor. The chatterbox is not only a pleasant talker, but also a person who amuses and is amused: they know how to laugh at themselves (thus distancing themselves from their true emotions), they know how to amuse and to make others laugh too, defending themselves in this way from being taken totally seriously.

When we inspect the observations of the classics in matters of character, we see that the portrait of the gluttonous character appears in Theophrastus under the name of "loquacity." When defining loquaciousness, Theophrastus, quite significantly employs a special word to capture this characterology: incontinence—in the sense of "verbal incontinence." He describes this type as one that is continuously talking and who does not give you a minute's peace.

> And when he has left a few (people) speechless, he is the one who then speaks to the groups and dedicates his time to distracting the people who have met to talk about a subject. He goes to the classrooms or to the wrestling school and bothers the students who are having lessons by gossiping with their teachers and trainers.

Evidently, the image that Theophrastus gives us is that of a person who not only talks too much, but also

---

[7] Elias Canetti, *Der Ohrenzeuge. Fünfzig Charaktere*, Carl Hanser Verlag, München 1979 (tr.: *Ear Witness: Fifty Characters*).

has a great need for contact, is narcissistic, and is lacking in tact with others:

"With his verbiage, he impedes the development of a trial or the contemplation of a spectacle at the theater or people from eating their dinner at ease ..."

With his loquacity, this man is hardly receptive, but he admits his defect and accepts the criticism of others. It is as if with this show of friendliness, he expects the same condescension on the part of his victims; a similar indulgence to his own.

We also find the chatterbox in the profile of Theophrastus's "news dealer." Nowadays, we see the news dealer in the person who is up to date with respect to the latest gossip or the latest academic publications. He or she therefore has information to offer in exchange for ears that listen. We see here how the gluttony of contact, attention, and appreciation are acquired by means of words.

It is clear that in the times of the *Commedia Dell'Arte*, this type of human was well known, and we find him in the likeable figure of Arlecchino. This is how Carla Poesio presents this character in her book on Italian masks.[8]

I am Arlecchino Batocio, from Bergamo, the humblest of servants of my lords. Who is this little man under the *tracagnotto*? He seems to be made of rubber, with his jumping and prancing around, with the pirouettes he mixes with his words. He uses a leather mask with two small holes for the eyes. He certainly is not handsome, but rather the opposite. Is he frightening? No! Look at the funny way he moves, his parrot-like voice, the lively expressions that he mixes with the nonsense that comes out of his mouth ... You don't know

---

[8]Op. cit.

whether he is a bit stupid or whether he pretends to be, and the trouble he stirs up is done without malice, and he is the one who ends up the most entangled of all. He does not have much of a desire to work, just a little, he is a servant by trade, who never finds a master who is content with him. His wages are often made up of potatoes and thrashings with a stick. Whether he merits them or not, that is the question. It's not my fault I'm ignorant, he sustains, and tells whoever wants to hear that when he was going to school a curious accident occurred: a cow ate his books with great relish. How could I interrupt such a substantial meal? I didn't have the courage. I let the cow eat the spelling book, the Pythagorean table, and all the other sources of science, down to the last page. Since that day on, poor thing, he has not been able to study. This may not be a good excuse, but the story works for Arlecchino, and he himself is the first to believe it ... One thing he is never without: hunger. He is eternally hungry. When he is finally about to fill the huge hole that he feels in his stomach—which seems to last him days, weeks, months—ninety times out of a hundred, something stands between him and his meal. And now he dreams. His name, *Arlecchino*, is derived from the word *lecchare* (to lick) in reference to hunger and gluttony. (He was probably first called *Lecchino* and then *Arlecchino*.)

Arlecchino
Illustration by Giorgio Sanson, © Edizioni Primavera, Florence

ENNEATYPE IV: ENVY

I have already explained that characters IV and V are to be found at the bottom of the enneagram, opposite character IX. I have characterized them as the most sensitive characters, those in which the sense of lack predominates, in contrast with the excessively satisfied character of those who repress their lacking and disconnect from their needing.

The fourth enneatype (EIV) is between EIII and EV. It is very like EV with respect to lacking, and its proximity to EIII may be understood if we consider that it resembles a frustrated form of vanity: these types of people tend to blame or belittle themselves. In contrast with EV, which is more intellectual, EIV is more emotional; while EV is retentive of its energy and participation, but unattached to people, EIV is attached to people.

This character may express envy in a "decapitating" way, according to the prototype of Cain, who competitively hated anyone else who had what he lacked—the rich, the male, the privileged. But there also exists admiring envy that spurs one on in a self-demanding desire to attain the social values or models which one feels to be deficient.

I have already explained, in relation to the masochistic character, the idea that attachment to suffering is this character's fundamental defect. This attachment is explained by a manipulative function of suffering. On the one hand, they use the maneuver of attracting love through the intensification of one's own need and frustration; they say: "A baby who does not cry, does not get (breast)fed." On the other hand, they place themselves in the role of the victim to serve the frustrated demand through making the other person guilty; something like:

"Look how I suffer because of you and understand what you owe me in the name of humanity and decency." The pain of the sufferers may also be understood as a transformation of hate—which becomes apparent pardon, while at the same time, from a position of sacrifice, they "destroy" the other person. Psychoanalysis has described this manner when talking about how the other becomes the "bad object."

Melanie Klein attributes not only envy to the suckling child, but also the fantasy of responding to frustration by transforming the "good object"—the mother's breast—into a "bad object" full of excrement. Whether such "projective identification" exists in the breastfed child or whether it is one of the "adultomorphic" interpretations of early childhood that Peterfreund[9] has criticized in his colleagues, it is still a good metaphor of debasement, from frustrated accusation, in the adult masochist.

Another characteristic defense mechanism of the envious person is "turning against the self" (rediscovered by Perls and called "retroflection" in the vocabulary of Gestalt therapy). It is applied especially to the unconscious aggression that becomes self-aggression. In no other human type is self-reproaching, self-hate, and self-destruction so present.

A third characteristic defense mechanism is introjection. Characterological masochism is so close to introjection that it may be understood as chronic self-poisoning, the result of having swallowed (in its excessive voracity) a "bad object." The situation is typically that of a rejecting mother that the person carries inside. In his or her desire for love, he or she seems to have given in to the unconscious fantasy that "swallowing" the other would

[9]*International Journal of Psychoanalysis*, 1978, 59, 427-441.

produce greater satisfaction, but only the opposite occurs.

Although Theophrastus does not have a portrait that is announced as the envious character, it is not difficult to recognize it in the character of his "whining" man[10], who, as we shall see, is also a pessimist.

> If a friend sends him a ration (of food) from a banquet, he tells the bearer: "I suppose that your master considers me unworthy of his soup and his wine, since he has not invited me to the feast." When his lover showers him with kisses, he says: "I find it strange that you love me with all your soul." If he has bought a slave at a good price due to having bargained insistently with the seller, he says to himself: "I'll be amazed if he is in good shape, being so cheap."

In the *Commedia Dell'Arte*, EIV is Pedrolino, the sad and lovesick clown better known to us as the French Pierrot. No less appropriate are the caricatures that William Steig has created in his book *Rejected Lovers* of the desperate musician and of a character who cries "Mommy" with a yearning expression of abandon, while he feels himself fall into the abyss.[11]

A profound observation of attachment to suffering and of the use of this to attract attention is reflected in the joke about the lady who is periodically heard to complain on a night train: "Oh my, I am so thirsty!" After some time, someone who cannot get to sleep gets up and gets her a glass of water. For a few moments there is silence and the passengers feel relieved, but then they hear: "How thirsty I was!"

---

[10]According to the cited edition, this character is described as "insatisfaction with one's lot." (Translator's Note in Spanish edition).
[11]William Steig, *Rejected Lovers*, Alfred A. Knopf, New York City: 1951, reprint by Dover Publications, Inc., 1973.

ENNEATYPE V: AVARICE

EV individuals seem to have concluded at the beginning of their lives that the world will not give them the love they yearn for, and they decide to fix things themselves, minimizing their desires. They distance themselves from the world, which asks more from them than it gives them and puts more impediments in their path rather than helps them—and to a certain extent "erases" them, forgets them. Like Hermann Hesse's Siddhartha, they seem to say to themselves: "I know how to wait, I know how to fast, I know how to think."

Quino has eloquently characterized the resigned self-denial that avarice entails in the cartoon (see following page) in which the emptiness of the surrounding space becomes a metaphor for emotional poverty.

Whereas some passions suppose moving towards the other too intensely, in this case we have a movement away from others. What Karen Horney said is very true: that the remote person can neither move *towards* the other via an amorous or seductive gesture nor *against* the other; in the conflict between these two tendencies—of love and aggression—he or she ends up departing the battle field. These types are neither warm nor ardent, but cool; however, their search for isolation and solitude, their desire not to be interfered with, invaded, subjected to demands, becomes a passion. What others search for outside of themselves, they search for inside, or beyond the interpersonal world—in the symbolic, the abstract, or the transcendental.

Not only is this a character that is close to fear, but also it has a form of this: a fear of ending up empty, of not having, of not being able. It entails a position of impotence and passivity with respect to life.

Gente en su sitio (People in their place)
© Quino, Editorial Lumen, Barcelona, 1986

74

It is also adjacent to envy, and one could say that it shares the sense of lacking with this character; but this is an envy paralyzed by fear, which instead of approaching the object of desire, renounces what it feels to be unreachable.

A great deal has been said in psychoanalysis about how schizoid people disconnect from their need for the other by means of the fantasy that their magnitude would be unacceptable, incompatible with life, that their voracity and dependence would lead them to "devour" the other. The fear of being devoured is likewise present: their own need would place these people in a situation in which the other used them, which is nonetheless true. When they enter into a relationship of dependence, they overadapt to the other to the extent that they forget their needs and need to reconnect with their inner world in solitude. Resignation arises on thinking that desiring is too much. Part of this character's makeup is to say to oneself: "Is it worth making an effort? Is it worth insisting?" There is a loss of intensity coupled to desperation. Resignation entails apathy. And this "Is it worth it?" is linked to their vision of the world. It seems to them that they are not going to find anything profoundly satisfactory. They anticipate being disappointed, as they were when they were small.

It may be said that a vicious circle is established by means of which the selfsame prohibition of avarice affords them an intensity that, in turn, redounds in its negation. The taboo of greed breeds greed, which in turn stimulates the prohibition of wanting nothing for oneself. The result is a guilty egoism that neither asks for anything nor accepts that it be given what it secretly desires. Something similar occurs with the desire for privacy: this is complicated with the laying of blame. The result is that in order to hide it from the other, this person ends up having to forget his or her own secret.

Apart from the resistance to *giving*, not *giving oneself* is typical of the "retentiveness" of this character, which is manifested in only being half committed to what one is doing, or in participating in things, while at the same time asking oneself whether it might not be better to save oneself for something else. They are likewise resistant to expressing themselves, particularly with respect to communicating emotions. Commitments are difficult, as a result of a desire to economize for a possible better investment of their energies. As a result, the avaricious person is a simple observer of life, hardly living it and wasting opportunities as well as talents.

The characteristic defense mechanism of this character is what Freud called "isolation," meaning the separation of some contents of the mind from others, as well as the compartmentalization or separation of ideas and feelings. The result is a good analytic capacity and a difficulty in seeing the overall aspect of situations and their meaning.

After defining meanness as "a lack of generosity with respect to spending," Theophrastus portrays the mean man in the following way:

> When voluntary donations are solicited in the assembly for the State, he silently gets up and disappears from the assembly ... On the feast in honor of the Muses, so as not to have to give any money, he stops his children from going to school on the pretext that they are ill ... He carries home the meat he has bought in the market himself and carries the vegetables in the fold of his gown. He stays at home when it is time to wash his cloak.

This image of the strictest economy of spending is a little more complex than the idea that might be considered *a priori*, since it suggests that this meanness not only indicates the desire not to spend and the sacrifice of personal desires in favor of avarice, but also a negation of the needs and desires of others. In virtue of this association, the word "meanness" not only speaks of economy, but more specifically of a lack of generosity in spending, as defined by Theophrastus.

As a distinction of meanness, Theophrastus speaks of avarice as "the desire to pursue a sordid profit" and gives a characterological portrait in which, together with these miserly traits, is to be found the covetous aspect of this type (which, in short, appears as disinterest and resignation):

> The person who suffers from this defect is capable, in a banquet he has organized, of not serving an adequate amount of bread and of asking the guest he has received in his house for a loan ... If he sells wine, even to a friend, he mixes it with water. He takes his children to the theater the day when entrance is free ... He makes his servant carry too much weight and to make things worse, he gives him less food than the other masters ... If he considers that one of his friends has bought something cheap, he buys it from him and resells it at a profit.

Among the characters of the *Commedia Dell'Arte*, perhaps the one that most evokes this character is one who seems to walk as if his feet did not touch the ground: Stenterello. The girls in the street laugh at his absent-mindedness, his clothes, and his appearance. Strange words and symbols cover his jacket as a sign of his interest for magic and mysterious knowledge. His name alludes to the poverty that accompanies his lack of worldliness.

A story by Pfeifer illuminates the way in which the hiding of desire in EV feeds passivity. He presents a subject who explains: "I live in a shell, which is inside a wall, which is inside a fortress, which is inside a tunnel, under the sea. I am safe and tranquil here. Safe from you. Tranquil that you are not going to disturb me." A woman rows past in a boat above all this, and he goes on to say: "If you really loved me, you would find me."

Up to now, we have spoken of two cheerful, charming characters, and then of two unsatisfied, problematic characters. We shall now tackle a third group—which includes Enneatypes I (Anger) and VIII (Lust)—made up of two aggressive characters: recognized aggression in one case (EVIII) and negated aggression in the other (EI).

Both EI and EVIII are domineering and are driven by a desire to conquer. But whereas EVIII takes an antisocial stance, such that rebellion against social norms acquires a positive value, the aggression in EI is rationalized.

ENNEATYPE VIII: LUST

An intense sexuality subject to the minimum restrictions is not the only thing that gives EVIII an excessive character. The consumption of energy, a liking for intense stimuli, an attraction to violence and risks, and an effusive manifestation of enthusiasm constitute alternative expressions of lust. Apart from being intense, lustful characters are strong people; as if toughness constituted for them a form of intensity: a shield that enables them to receive the strongest blows.

Intensity and toughness would seem to be opposites. Intensity suggests life; toughness is a form of death. Although they may be opposites, the fact that they coexist reveals an intimate relationship: the intense, "Dionysian" aspect of the character may be understood as overcompensation for a secret insensitivity. The great vitality of EVIII is the expression of a passion; the demonstration of being alive on the part of someone who suffers from a kind of psychic callousness. At the same time, the search for intensity through pleasure and power leads to desensitization—since triumph demands invulnerability and desensitization with respect to the consequences that one's own gratification has for others.

Ichazo designated the "fixation" of EVIII as revenge, coinciding in this with Karen Horney's emphasis in her description of aggressive winners. But the revenge we are dealing with here must not be confused with the visible revenge that we usually associate with the term: it does not refer to taking revenge today because of what happened yesterday, but rather the instantaneous revenge of the person who responds to aggression with aggression, and a continuous, long-term revenge in response to the situation of childhood suffering. Just as the original frustration was linked to the weakness and relative impotence of childhood, the main strategy will subsequently be that of taking over power: having to dominate the situation, being on top, displaying strength. It is a strategy of the bully, of relying on force. While the contraphobic character seeks a power-authority that is based on ongoing blaming, here we are dealing with a power-to-do that is, in turn, based on ongoing threatening. While the tendency in EVI culminates in megalomania, resulting in the individual becoming a powerful giant, the culmination of the anxiety for power of EVIII is criminal abuse.

In my book *Ennea-type Structures*[12], I described this character somewhat picturesquely by the expression "Coming on Strong," which alludes to an overpowering expansiveness. The idea was inspired by a caricature of a girl who makes her boyfriend fall off his chair without realizing how.

These are characters that ride roughshod over others and who are not aware most of the time that they are doing so. They simply learned very early on in life that to get things it was necessary to assert themselves and to get down to work. This excessively active character, which is such a far cry (in his or her exaggerated autonomy) from the pathology of dependent characters, is also pathological in so far as dependence is negated. Wilhelm Reich already described a "phallic-narcissistic" character. As this expression suggests, this is not only someone who is hard and lustful, but also someone with a characteristic exhibitionist tendency. However, the exhibition of power or superiority of this character differs profoundly from vanity, since it constitutes more a means at the service of practical triumph rather than practical triumph at the service of applause. No one is bothered as little by what others think of them.

The defense mechanisms of EVIII are negation—a type of negation of pain—and psychological discomfort, which I have proposed to call simply "desensitization." The following anecdote may explain this last term. On a trip to Mexico, at dawn Nasruddin comes across a man with a dagger stuck in his chest lying in a pool of blood under the weak light of a street lamp. Somewhat alarmed, he asks him if he is suffering a lot, and the tough guy replies: "Only when I laugh, buddy."

---

[12]Gateways Books and Tapes, Nevada City, California, 1990, 2004.

As far as what can be appreciated in Theophrastus's *Characters*, this type must have been pretty common in the 3rd century B.C., since among the thirty characterizations in this collection, there are six descriptions that fit forms of the lustful type, many more than those that I can find matching other types of the Enneagram.

He calls one of these the "bold cynic,"[13] and defines him as a person capable of having the cheek to do or say shameful things:

> The cynic (shameless person) is a type of man who swears an oath lightly, has a bad reputation and insults the powerful. He has a vulgar character and is capable of anything. You can be sure he does not mind dancing the córdace[14], without being drunk and without wearing a mask in a procession.

Theophrastus's definition of cynicism (or shamelessness) falls short in comparison to his description, as he portrays a character that not only attributes little importance to the opinions of others, but also is not upset by any pursuit, no matter how loathsome it may be. He also tells us that "he let his elderly mother die of hunger," which shows us his lack of human feelings and generalized hostility. He likewise affirms that the cynic (or shameless person) "is arrested for robbery and spends the best part of his life in prison rather than at home," which

---

[13]In the cited Spanish version, the "bold cynic" appears as "shameless person," and Theophrastus defines this as a boldness that manifests itself in reprehensible acts and words (Spanish edition translator's note).

[14]I cite the same note that appears in this version: "A primitive religious dance related to the origins of comedy, characterized by its violent movements and wild abandon, being considered by many authors of Antiquity to be licentious and shameful." (Spanish edition translator's note).

81

reflects a clear indifference to public opinion and the welfare of others. In short, his disposition is antisocial.

In this last portrait we find another important trait of the character: exhibitionism, also characteristic of EVIII.

> He could be one of those who gather around themselves and convoke a circle of people and then, with a powerful, cavernous voice, apostrophize and strike up a conversation with them[15] ... He finds no better occasion to make a show of his cynicism (shamelessness) than when there is a public feast.

Theophrastus tells us that the cynic (shameless person) "is a tavern keeper, acts as a pimp or is a tax collector" and that "he usually does the rounds of the taverns, the fishmongers' and the salting shops, and he guards the profit he obtains from this tax collecting in his mouth."

All this reflects a trait that Theophrastus chooses as a name for another of his characters: "the rabble's friend."[16] Once more, his definition here is not as complex as the attributes that he suggests literally: a liking for associating with people of low standing and subjects who are looked down on by the refined and those who accept the law.

He tells us that "'To be a friend of the rabble' (a liking for wickedness) simply means an inclination for the perverse." The character he mentions could just as well

---

[15]This could also be: "He is one of those people who attracts the crowd and harangues, scolds or converses with them in a loud gruff voice." (translator's note in Spanish edition).
[16]In the cited version, this appears as "a liking for wickedness." (Spanish edition translator's note).

describe the cynic (shameless person), since the latter has a view of things that supposes a cynical (shameless) invalidation of the values of daily life.

> If honest folk speak, he maintains that honesty is unnatural and that all men are unequal, and he recriminates those who are honest. He affirms with total tranquility that the wicked man is one who has freed himself of prejudices.

In the observation that Theophrastus makes about his defense of the oppressed, we can see something more than rebellion and cynicism (shamelessness). There is also an implicit vindictive spirit in his sense of justice and something of genuine empathy, as we shall have the opportunity to discover (in spite of the fact, from what we have seen previously, that he does not have the least empathy at all for his own mother).

Theophrastus speaks of the lack of scruples as "indifference with respect to the reputation of interest in obtaining loathsome profit," and affords us a general image of this type in which his indifference with respect to his reputation stands out, though now in the company of profit, which, in short, is to talk of greed.

Close to this character in the portrait gallery, we find that of the "coarse" person:

> Coarseness is not difficult to define; it is annoying, disagreeable mockery ... The coarse person is the type of subject who, when he finds himself among respectable women, lifts up his clothes to exhibit his genitals ... He stops in front of the barber's or the perfume shop and tells the customers that he is going to get drunk.

Finally, we can encounter the stamp of Enneatype VIII in the "bad-mannered"[17] type. "The bad-mannered person is one who, if asked the question: Who is this? replies: Don't start bothering me! It is obvious that the person thus described is not only bad mannered, but also distrustful: "He tells those who show him signs of esteem and send him some kind of present that they are up to something." He is also hostile. "He is incapable of forgiving someone who accidentally dirties his clothes, pushes him, or treads on his foot."

Among the Italian masks we find EVIII embodied in Brighella, a fairground charlatan whose advice is that lies should be like meatballs: *big*.

> Brighella has bright, malicious eyes under a leather mask, thick lips and a turned up mustache and is dressed in white.
> If my clothes are white, says Brighella, that means that I have carte blanche to do and undo as I please. And the green adornments? Ah, that's something else altogether. The desires of my customers will always remain green: that is to say, unsatisfied. I may make promises, but another thing is keeping them.
> His name, Brighella Cavicchio, derives from briga, deception, trick, something not very clear, and also evokes the first two syllables of brigand. He is a character that comes down to us from the 14th century, from Upper Bergamo, reputed for its astute folk, while in Lower Bergamo are to be found simple, good-natured types, more like Arlecchino or Pulcinella, who though they cause trouble, do so with good intentions, poor devils, to get themselves out of trouble.
> The case of Brighella is different. He deceives others for pleasure; he is great at cooking up ruses: he makes

---

[17]This "bad-mannered" person appears in the cited version as rude (Spanish edition translator's note).

them big and decorated like a wedding cake.

This is the way he shamelessly proclaims in the market place: I have talismans for everything, perfectly triangular stones, collected from faraway India, that safeguard from all dangers those who possess one, I also prepare magnetic dressings that cure rheumatism or liver sickness in twenty-four hours, I make lotions for the bald and magic filters for young women looking for a husband.

Brighella laughs at the people at the fair, at those sitting in the market place, at the credulous servants and their elderly masters."[18]

---

[18]Carla Poesio, op. cit.

Brighella
Illustration by Giorgio Sansoni
© Edizioni Primavera, Florence

ENNEATYPE I: ANGER

The fact that the defense mechanism of the obsessive character is "reactive formation," which through compensation transforms psychological contents into their opposites, means that the anger of the irate constitutes a less visible passion than the pride of the proud or the lust of the lustful. While the envious may not wish to see their envy, thus negating it, or those who are very afraid of being afraid ignore their fear, the negation of anger in the perfectionist character seems to be an especially accusatory case of unconsciousness, and makes the term "irate" particularly inept for suggesting the apparent personality of its bearer.

The "irate" person is one who typically acts the part of the "good boy or girl" in life. In today's world, he or she is often a pacifist. An "irate" mother probably will not like her son to have war toys or lead soldiers. The aggressive potential in her psyche is overcompensating for something much more apparent: the ethical mandate of non-aggression. And the perfectionist character is usually that of a moralist, and if not, that of a person whose enthusiasm for rules, norms, good intentions, and noble resolutions stand out. For no one else is the following refrain so appropriate: "The road to hell is paved with good intentions."

I have sometimes described this character as that of "angry virtue," an expression that reflects both the passionate-emotional aspect of the character and this type's "fixation" or mistaken perspective on life: the idea that one is worth nothing nor is one worthy of love unless one is perfect. This leads this person, so characteristically devoted, and an advocate of good, to be excessively critical and not at all affectionate. To be able to love only what is perfect is truly a form of not being able to love.

The self-image of a good person, however, is maintained by a continuous diet of good intentions and good works, and by the rationalization of perfectionist anger as a noble battle in the name of higher ideals.

There are perfectionists who identify more with their idealized image than with their denigrated image and therefore feel superior due to their excellence, while at the same time undervaluing their fellow men. The expression *Holier than Thou* is fitting here: it refers to the tendency to exalt one's own nobility and to see the plebeian or uncultivated aspect of others in an exaggerated manner. The English have been caricatured for their excessive inclination to feel that they are in the right and to perceive others as savages, particularly in the days of their empire and colonies. This variant corresponds to rigid characters that expect the whole world to adapt to them, to listen to them, and to imitate their noble example, in so far as they identify with their idealized self.

Others, in comparison, criticize themselves more; they have greater contact with their denigrated self. What strikes one most of all about these EI people is their respect for the excellence of others, as well as their diminished tendency to set themselves up as an authority, in contrast with the rigid. These are people whose perfectionism never allows them to become satisfied; they never feel that they have done things well enough to be at peace with themselves. We can characterize them as worried individuals.

When we move from the religious discourse to the observation of human life made by the writers who have specialized in character analysis, we can observe that the personality syndrome that we are dealing with here has been studied since Antiquity, though not in the sense that we nowadays call "psychodynamics."

Among his characters, Theophrastus describes one whom he calls "the oligarch," and defines oligarchy as "the desire for control that aspires to power and riches." The oligarch portrayed here goes beyond an aristocratic combination of presumptuousness, refinement, and unrecognized dominance. He tells us that he constantly uses certain phrases, expressions that allude to aristocratic feelings, disdain, and ceremony.

> We ought to get together, just ourselves, and make decisions concerning these matters, avoiding the crowd and the *agora*. Let us put an end to our participation in magistracy, and thus to the criticisms and honors of this rabble. This city must be governed by them or by us ... The oligarch never goes out before midday; his cloak is carefully draped, his beard neat and tidy and his fingernails properly cut. ... They dislike sitting in the assembly next to a subject who is dressed in rags.

In the spectrum of *Commedia Dell'Arte* characters, EI is manifest in Pantalone—the authoritarian old nobleman that seems to have originated in the more ancient *senex*: the unpleasant critical old man already ridiculed since Roman comedy. The plots of stories involving Pantalone emphasize his repressive control over his astute servant Arlechino and most attractive maid Colombina. His appearance is shown in the dagger-bearing bearded figure in the illustration on page 90.

Such pedantry and distraction from what is essential is reflected by the anecdote of the Frenchman who, just before dying, states: *"Je meure"* ("I die"). Or, *"Je me meure"* ("I die myself")—which may be said in both forms.

Pantalone
Illustration by Georio Sansoni
© Edizioni Primavera, Florence

90

ENNEATYPE IX: INDOLENCE

Indolence or psychological laziness is also spiritual inertia, and EIX entails not only a not wanting to know, an "ostrich policy," but also overstability, a resistance to change. This is, in general, a person who is overadapted to the desires of others, overly complacent, and with scant initiative. His or her inner state resembles going around half asleep, half dead to life. This is a dispassionate, phlegmatic character, though the switching off of his or her personal desires frequently coincides with a jovial, gregarious disposition. In human relations, however, this is an overly self-sacrificing person, overly resigned, passive, conformist; generally a simple person, "without problems"—apart from his or her excessive intolerance of troubles and excessive difficulty when it comes to saying "no," which often makes these people a target for exploitation.

It would appear that there is less to say about EIX than the other characters in view of the great simplification of their psychological life. Their tendency to forget their own needs due to excessive complacence apparently coincides with the Christian ideal, and not bothering anyone does not have a clear place in the current diagnostic categories of aberrant personalities. One of the defense mechanisms that characterizes this type (which Freud called "altruistic self-postponement") has even been considered less pathological than others in virtue of its social function. But the advantage of EIX (just like the disadvantage of Enneatypes IV and V, at the other pole of the Enneagram) is more apparent than real, since these people's automatic, compulsive altruism does not make them ethically better than others. Actually, it might be said that destructiveness is less visible in this character.

In his description of the "dim man," Theophrastus calls our attention to a cognitive laziness that is characteristic of Enneatype IX, with intellectual, as well as spiritual, befuddlement: "Dimness might be defined as a slowness of the mind with respect to words and actions."

Some of the examples that he includes in his description refer to absent-mindedness; others reflect not only the lack of attention, but also the lack of intellectual interest. "If he goes to the theater, he falls asleep and when the play is over, everyone leaves and he remains alone in the theater." This behavior of the "dim man" in particular may also be interpreted as a lack of cultural sophistication, which is the consequence of intellectual laziness and concreteness that leads to another character that Theophrastus calls "rusticity."

Though he defines "rusticity" as ignorance, lacking in manners, his portrait suggests something very close to a closed mentality. He emphasizes the narrowness of interests, an excess of concreteness, and the limiting of life in favor of functionality. He also alludes implicitly not just to a simple lack of refinement, but to despiritualization:

> He wears shoes that are bigger than his feet and speaks in a loud, booming voice. He distrusts friends and relatives and entrusts his most important secrets to his servants ... He neither stops nor makes inquiries in the street for any other reason; but, however, he stands and stares when he sees an ox, an ass, or a billy goat.

Among the Italian masks, Enneatype IX is to be recognized in that of Gianduia. Carla Poesio explains in her book as follows:

> Nowadays there exists a kind of chocolate bar called *gianduiotto* in honor of Gianduia, an old mask from Piamonte, and they are called so after the Giandujott,

the children of Gianduia. It is difficult to find a boy who is gayer, healthier, more pleased with his lot. Maybe because they are peasants. His mother Giacometta and his father Gianduia have given rise to a very large family. It is difficult to know how many Giandujott there are.

He likes to visit the different inns of the city and his humor and gaiety entertains those present. He is not handsome but is pleasant. Plump and tanned, with a slightly naïve expression, it is always easy to make fun of him.

Gianduia
Illustration by Georio Sansoni
© Edizioni Primavera, Florence

ENNEATYPE III: VANITY

The current use of the word "vanity" corresponds to the image with which Catholic iconography represents pride or *superbia*: a woman looking at herself in the mirror. But the physical image is not the only possible focus of the desire to present a good image. The desire to shine in the social world or the desire for financial success certainly has more social repercussions. What is more, the desire to shine and to have more success entails the development of an ability, and goes hand in hand with an active, practical, expedient, and efficient disposition that is also characteristic of this style of personality.

Excessive vanity implies an excessive orientation according to outside values; what is socially valued becomes more important and the person becomes tremendously imitative, "mimetic." Besides, conformity to exterior models implies the development of great control over oneself, which leads to superficiality. The North American sociologist David Riesman has described this phenomenon, which he calls other-directedness (extrinsic orientation). Curiously enough, this is a character that does not appear in the North American diagnostic manual DSM-III. This is understandable, since these are happy, extravert, and pleasant characters for those around them.

Erich Fromm, however, focuses on this character, as I have previously explained, with his concept of "marketing orientation." Fromm's thesis, according to which this is a character that has arisen in the modern world due to the influence of the market, does not seem acceptable to me. Clearly Theophrastus knew this type of vain person.

Theophrastus included both the cases of those worried about shining and status as well as other, more specific cases whose preference is to keep their hair short and their teeth clean and white.

Citing his text:

Vanity is the unhappy desire for distinction.[19] The vain man is one who when invited to dinner wants to sit next to the host. He takes his son to have his hair cut in Delphos. He has a black slave who accompanies him on his walks. When he pays a silver *mina*, he makes sure he does so with new coins. He has a tame rook at home for which he has bought a ladder and has had a little bronze shield made, so that it can jump up the steps. If he sacrifices an ox, he nails the head to the door to his house, so that the whole world can see that he has sacrificed an ox. ... He gets his fellow members of the assembly of honor to announce to his fellow citizens the result of the sacrifice and he dresses for the occasion in a white tunic with a garland on his head. He climbs up to the tribune and proclaims: 'Athenians, we the senators have made the due sacrifices in honor of the Mother of the Gods. The omens are favorable.' And when he has made his proclamation, he goes home to announce to his wife the incredible success he has reaped. He has his hair cut frequently and takes care that his teeth are really white; he changes his clothes, even though they are in good condition and he is well perfumed. In the *agora*, he frequents the tables of the bankers; he frequents the gymnasiums in which the youth train; in the theater he sits near the people who hold important positions.

He buys nothing for his personal use, but rather for his foreign friends: olives for Byzantium, Spartan dogs

---

[19]In the text in Spanish in the cited version, instead of this affirmation, it states literally "mean desire for ostentation." (Spanish edition translator's note).

for Cyzicus, and Hymmetian honey for Rhodes. This way, all the city is informed about his acts.

He possesses a small gymnasium with a court for ball games, and he goes around the city inviting sophists, fencing masters, and musicians to perform there; and he makes sure to arrive late at the exhibition so that people can say: He is the owner of the gymnasium.

The fundamental defect of the vain is falseness, inauthenticity, their confusion between the image they offer to the world and their actual reality. More than a falsification of facts, this falseness entails a particular viewpoint about themselves. In contrast to the proud, who exaggerate their merits, here we have confusion with respect to value criteria, which are external and excessively concrete. This is the kind of mind referred to by the Little Prince when he speaks of adults who like numbers a lot, who ask how old you are and how much you earn, though it would never occur to them to ask whether you collect butterflies.

A prominent defense mechanism in this character is negation, by means of which they affirm something that is not true in order to distract (themselves) from the awareness of what is. Their tendency to identify is also marked, particularly in the sense of modeling themselves in an imitative manner around extrinsic patterns.

Among the Italian masks, we find the character of Florindo. Carla Poesio says of him:

> Is he intelligent or stupid, brave or vain, is he ignorant or wise, this gentleman dressed so elegantly, with a velvet tricorn decorated with small, costly feathers that is so well-positioned by the hand of an expert on his curly wig? It is not so easy to know, it depends on the occasion. Maybe it is not of interest to know. What

can be said without doubt is that he is handsome and elegant, that he chooses well his words, his gestures, and how he is dressed. He seems made for the role of the lover. We shall ask no more.

His fingers are weighed down with rings, across his belly hangs a chain with many pendants and two watches. Yes, two; because this gentleman wants people to see that he always has the exact time, as he can control this with one more watch than the single one common to others.

Before the ladies he is most ceremonious. Notice what a masterpiece his way of inclining is—he places one hand over his heart while with the other he describes a wide semi-circle with his feathered tricorn.

His eloquence is made up of complicated discourses, of well-chosen words, that surpass everyday language.

Florindo
Illustration by Georio Sansoni
© Edizioni Primavera, Florence

ENNEATYPE VI: COWARDICE

Surely fear has been known in all ages. The description that I know that most approaches a technical description, as a result of the context within which it occurs, is the coward in Theophrastus's characters.

After defining cowardice as "a certain deficiency of spirit caused by fear," Theophrastus describes the coward to us as the person who when he makes a voyage:

> ... confuses the coastal cliffs with pirate ships and from the moment the sea gets rough asks the crew if they have experience in sailing ... He tells the person sitting next to him that he had a dream involving bad omens the previous night ... and finally begs to be disembarked. In the course of a military expedition, and when the infantry enters into combat ..., he says to his comrades that with all the haste he has forgotten his sword; he runs back to his tent and hides his sword under the pillow and lets a long time pass as if he were looking for it ... If he sees a friend being brought back wounded, he runs to him, encourages him and puts his friend's arm over his own shoulder and helps carry him. He then attends him and cleans the blood from his wounds and, seated at his bedside, swats away the flies. In other words, he does everything apart from fighting against the enemy. When the trumpet sounds the call to arms, he protests, seated in the tent, saying: 'Go take a walk, don't you see you aren't letting this poor man sleep due to the racket you are making.' Covered in the blood of the other man, he leaves the tent to go in search of the soldiers who are returning from the battlefield and tells them he has saved one of their comrades, as if he had put his own life in danger.

Though Theophrastus could not make the mistake of omitting the coward in his gallery of aberrant characters, Enneatype VI is related not only to cowardice, but also to superstition (a theme of another of his characters) as an element that is particularly associated with the openly fearful individual, in comparison with the aggressive and rigid variants of this enneatype. Theophrastus is aware of the connection between superstition and fear when he says: "Superstition might simply be cowardice with respect to the supernatural."

Examples of the contraphobic form of the suspicious character are Captain Ahab in *Moby Dick* and Macbeth, who lives on guard against imaginary attacks due to his secret guilt. These are combative people who generally do not know that there is fear in their combativeness and their pugnacity, and who appear to others to be moved by extraordinary bravery.

Another form of distrustful character, which I have called the "Prussian character," is typical of those who act according to hierarchical terms, with an implicit fear of not doing their duty or what a certain code, ideology, or faith requires. This kind of individual is usually called a *true believer,* a fanatic. While others doubt, they protect themselves against doubt like Quixotes, who attract the attention of the "Sanchos" in particular since, from the latters' viewpoint, they are raving lunatics.

The fear of making mistakes, which in the timid manifests as excessive submission, evasion of the responsibility of deciding, hesitation and excessive caution, and which in the strong—contraphobic—manifests as aggressivity, here leads to an obsessive devotion to grandiose ideals.

The principal defect behind the emotional climate of suspicion is what could be called "self-demonization": self-accusation that implies a guilty view of oneself. The actual fear is implicitly a fear of transgression, of guilt, of punishment and condemnation that implies going beyond what is prescribed by a tacit authority in the inner world.

It may be said that the merging of authority and accusation in this character constitutes a bad authority, an aggressive authority that is opposed to the good of the subject and points to a defense mechanism described by Anna Freud as "identification with the aggressor"; namely, to defend oneself from external aggression by incorporating it. So as not to be in dissonance with it, these individuals assume the judgment of the accuser in an act that results in complete self-squelching.

By way of complementing the dramatic descriptions from literature and psychopathology, here are some humorous vignettes. As an illustration of the hesitating, suspicious type, there is the story that says when you meet a Galician on the stairs, you never know if he is going up or down, and this type replies suspiciously to whoever questions: "And why do you wish to know that?" The caricature of the strong, suspicious (contraphobic) character is Popeye, with his invulnerability, his muscles, and pop-eyes (from which his name obviously proceeds).

Among the Italian masks, Captain Spavento is determined to show how handsome, powerful, fearful, and above all, how brave he is. In contrast with others, he does not wear a mask, but does have a ferocious expression, as well as a turned-up mustache that seems to "punch holes in the sky." He says he is a great soldier, but in fact he is a braggart, who prefers telling imaginary tales of battles to actually fighting. He is known by different names: Iron Spitter, Big Bombardier, Fire Blood, Moor Slayer, Captain Crocodile.

Captain Spavento
Illustration by Georio Sansoni
© Edizioni Primavera, Florence

Whatever the ventures of this character, only he can narrate them, because no one has ever seen him fight against a true enemy. This is the way he threatens an adversary: "If I kick your butt, I'll send you all the way to Turkey, if not burn your hair in the sphere of the Sun."

He is often represented together with a servant, Fagiolo, who pretends to listen attentively to his sword thrusts. This servant remarks, for instance, that he hears him say: "Tremble, enemies, because your blood shall quench the thirst of my sword!"

FACING THE TRUTH

Sayed Omar Ah Shah—known as "the Agha"—affirms that we already know that some people are idiots and others are cowards or liars, but it is not necessary to go around saying so. I have no doubt, however, that it better serves the common good to do so. I have always felt enormous gratitude to the "masters of the stick," without whom we perhaps might not take benefit from what we are offered by the masters of love.

One of the most outstanding gifts of Gurdjieff, abundantly known to those who were lucky enough to surround him, was his capacity to confront people with their hard truths. Perhaps the main similarity between the school of Gurdjieff and that of Ichazo (who called himself "master of the sword") was a day-to-day war against the *ego*, and the theory of Protoanalysis within the context of his work fed a process of mutual, continuous "*ego* reduction."

Recently, some people say that it is better not to think about the bad aspects of oneself and to concentrate on what is positive. More concretely, they say that too much emphasis has been placed in the presentation of the enneagram of characters on what is negative without paying equal attention to the "positive traits" of human types. Such an attitude can only come from individuals who do not understand the enormous transforming value of this knowledge, which, leaving aside the care that these people take with respect to their image and their self-importance, is used to examine oneself and not merely to increase one's culture or congratulate oneself.

My book *Ennea-type Structures*, cited above, has been called a work tool. I would like this chapter, though brief, also to facilitate the self-knowledge of my readers. In the world of professional psychology, we commonly say that one cannot know oneself without outside help, and the tradition through which the Enneagram reaches us affirms that it is impossible to know one's own fundamental trait. I hope that, faced with a mirror as elaborated as the collage of portraits and comments on the preceding pages, the reader will find this no longer as true.

III

The Disturbances of Love

THE UNNAMED MYSTERY

After I gave a talk on "the ills of love and the ills of the world" at the University of Deusto some months ago, a member of the audience complained that I had not offered a definition of love. After having talked for more than an hour about what love is not, I thought: Isn't this in fact worth more than a definition? Wasn't it more elegant to leave the mystery unnamed, without going into fancy rationalist arguments? And I had to stop myself from responding: "Is a definition of God given in the Gospels?"

If I am not mistaken, St. John affirms that God is love. The task of a preliminary definition is certainly not an easy one. I recall the observation of Idries Shah about a man who taught that "trees were good." He had decided that all of perfection and beauty was contained in trees, which gave fruit, refuge and raw materials for craftsmen, without making any demands. His followers loved trees and adored woods and forests for ten thousand years, and Shah commented that these people confused what is immediate with what is real, in the same way that man is confused with respect to his present ideas about love:

"His most sublime ideas about love, if only he knew it, may be considered the lowest ideas about love in his present ideals."[1]

Even though I make no attempt at a definition of love that reveals its essential nature, it seems opportune to observe that, if it is legitimate to conceive of love as something beyond its various forms, this will be something common to a series of different experiences that we do not hesitate to call love. What do the love between sexes, motherly love, the admiring love of a friend, and benevolence towards a colleague or schoolmate have in common? I shall simply indicate that three experiences, three different loves—erotic attraction, benevolence, and admiration—in their transformations and varied combinations, constitute unquestionable manifestations of love life. If we wish to go further, we can only resort to words like "affirmation" or "attribution of value," which fall short in spite of the fact that we have nothing better.

The love that such a high proportion of literature and the cinema poeticizes is certainly not the same love referred to by the Christian commandment to love our neighbor as ourselves. At least, there is a sufficiently distinct emphasis that has enabled the philosophers of love always to have distinguished between *amor* per se and *caritas* (charity), or—to pass from Latin to Greek—*eros* and *agape*: one love that is associated with sexuality and is expressed above all in the mutual attraction between

---

[1]Idries Shah, *Reflexiones*, Paidós, Barcelona, 1986.

sexes, and another that is independent of sexuality, whose protoypical manifestation lies in the mother-child feeding relationship. Irrespective of whether amorous relationships exist in which both ingredients are present, and regardless also of whether there is a relationship between these two loves (such that compassion may feed sexuality, as in the Tantric path), it is true the two phenomena may be independent or antagonistic—as is typical in Christian culture, in which the principle of *agape* occurs in an ascetic context.

But this duality does not embrace the full spectrum of love. If compassionate love, the echo of maternal love, is a love that gives, and purely erotic love is a desire-love that yearns to receive, there is also an adoration-love that both gives and receives: it bestows its affirmation on the beloved and feeds on the radiance of the Divinity that it discovers, and in turn nurtures, via its act of adoration.

Hubert Benoit states that adoration-love always involves—to a greater or lesser extent—the projection onto a you of the image of the divine. I agree, but I do not share with him the identification of adoration-love with erotic love, no matter how much it constitutes the essence of falling in love. I think that falling in love is the result of a convergence between erotic and admiring love, and that admiring-love has its prototypical form in the relationship between a small boy and his father rather than with his mother (with respect to whom his experience is more one of pleasure-love or eros than receiving-love). Also, from Socratic love to the *Summum Bonum* may be said to be a hybrid between wisdom and erotic attraction. Admiring-love—particularly present in the masculine love that Plato called *philia*—does not necessarily feed on *eros*, as demonstrated by the devotion to a spiritual master or as Nietzsche pointed out:

"Woman loves man and man loves God."

There is some truth in all this, in so far as there exists a love that entails a disinterested giving of self, a love for something that is neither oneself (like desire-love) nor another (like giving-love), and which may be called "love of God" in the broad sense of the expression—whether it be love of beauty, of justice, of good, or of life.

Eros (or desire-love), *caritas/agape* (or giving-love) and *philia* (or admiring-love) may be characterized as the love of the child, the love of the mother, and the love of the father. These are predominantly related to the first, second, and third persons that distinguish the structure of our language: desire-love, with its yearnings to receive, privileges the I, while *agape*-love is a love of you, and admiring-love projects the valuing experience beyond the I-you experience, in a personification of that which is transcendendent or a symbolization of pure value: He. It may also be said that love of I embraces the inner animal that exists in us, a creature of desires, while the love of you approaches the other like a person or human being, and admiring-love encounters its true object in the divine—whether in a universal dimension or in the experience of incarnate divinity.[2]

It may likewise be said that love of the animal self is related to our instinct of conservation; our human love or our love of you constitutes the flourishing of sexuality; and our love of supreme values connects not only with the paternal, but also with the process of socialization and the social instinct that seeks relationship for relationship itself.

It is clear that each of these three loves can degenerate. Thus, for instance, alongside *eros*, which the Greeks

[2]This analysis echoes that proposed by Raimundo Panikkar in his examination of the Christian Triad, *The Threefold Linguistic Intrasubjectivity*, Archivio di Filosofia, 1986, no. 1-3, 593-6.

so aptly personified as a god, there is an eroticism prompted by lack. Rather than an instinct, this should be understood as an instinctive derivative or a reflection of instinctivity: a search for pleasure motivated by the difficulty of finding it; a hedonism that covers up and wishes to compensate unhappiness. We can characterize this excess and falsification of *eros* as irresponsible love.

Freud identifies *eros* and *libido*, but given the current usage of the term "libido" to mean the psychological fuel of neurosis—this "inverse love" that seeks itself in the dark—it would be better to reserve *eros* for love itself, which is an expression of abundance and a phenomenon of brimming over that accompanies the fullness of being.

The child goes from receiving-love to the capacity to give, or at least we may assume that this is healthy development. In the majority of cases, however, the individual remains fixated in necessity: early frustration becomes chronic and takes up the psychological energies of the adult. As he or she does not know what it is to receive, the person does not know how to give. Receiving-love or *libido* therefore not only absorbs the *eros* of pleasure-love, but also eclipses giving-love and admiring-love.

Love of one's neighbor, on the other hand, is particularly well known to us through its degraded form: hypocrisy. And bad love always entails an aspect of falsification; passing off one thing for another, saying "this is love." But apart from its aspect of false love, love also entails an anti-love: an exploitive voracity. The falsification of love supposes a particular illusion of over-identification of love with some other associated, overvalued experience such as pleasure or what is admirable or the gift of one's own subordination.

Admiring-love is in turn the root of comparable excesses when the *nomos* or amorous moral norm is transformed into authoritarian legalism. No matter how much people talk about love of God or one's country, they in fact talk in the name of love with the voice of obligation. Social movements and the anxiety of individuals for power feed this obliging-love.[3]

The insufficiencies of receiving love, of giving love, and of admiring love are naturally as well-known as their social excesses.

Whereas in the Law of Moses the first and most important precept is to love God, there is no place for the love of God in scientific psychology, which scarcely accepts the concept of "love" in its vocabulary (preferring objective concepts such as "positive emotional reinforcement"). Perhaps God has come to appear irrelevant to us after centuries of naming Him in vain and of degrading the idea of God via association with fossilized authoritarian religious institutions. For this reason, I wish to affirm my conviction that emotional health implies a "love of God" in the broad sense of the word, independent of all ideology and even compatible with agnosticism. When, for instance, someone asked the elderly Buber if he believed in God, he replied something like this: "If God is something that is independent of me, I don't know; if he is someone with whom I can enter into a relationship, yes."

The Christian commandment to "love your neighbor as yourself, and God above all things" does not refer in fact to one single love, but to a balance between *three* loves: of I, of you, and of Him. And it is not a question of loving one's neighbor *more* than oneself, but of loving the *human being*—both in others and in oneself—and loving even more that which is greater than human.

---

[3]It is significant that love of the living earth and humanity is formulated as a love of the "fatherland" rather than a "motherland."

Of course, many fail to fulfill this spiritual principle because of egoism or scant love for their neighbor. Rather than a brother, the other becomes a stranger who is ignored, used, or fought. This love entails a loss of *you*, a loss of the capacity to feel the other as a subject.

It would appear that the essence of egoism is love of oneself; but if we closely examine the psychological situation of egoism, we see that it entails above all a passionate search for substitutes for self and love. More than a form of self love, it is the result of an implicit rejection of oneself. Because the egoist does not love him or herself, he or she needs to fill this vacuum with an exaltation of secondary desires. The condition of friendship or benevolence with oneself is different from instinct: not an impulse, but a generous affirmation of the impulse; not animal motivation, but intimate human experience.

But failure exists not only with respect to human love, particularly in our secular world. I think that a fundamental aspect of many pathological conditions is the loss of this love that goes beyond the love for one's neighbor and the love for oneself. I think it is something like a burning of the divine spark that is within us, loving itself. It is from this love without an object, or whose object is infinite, that the density of the sense of life mainly derives, its "meaning," over and above all reason and interpersonal emotions.

Part of my analysis of "bad love"—as the archpriest would call it—will consist in a consideration of the diverse characters in terms of the three loves: a paternal love (*philia*, oriented towards the divine), a maternal love (*agape*, projected onto one's fellow man), and a form of love related to childlikeness (*eros*, focused on desire). The rest of this essay gives a broader treatment of how love in each of the neurotic styles is hindered, falsified, or betrayed.

St. Thomas suggested distinguishing between the aspects in sin he calls *aversio* and *conversio*: separation from God and exaggerated attraction to the world. We find this thought echoed in Dante's *Divine Comedy* in the doctrine that each of the capital sins entails a different deviation from love—for Dante, sins are forms of love that, blind to their True object and to themselves, are fascinated by reflections and mirages.

Although my intention to treat the illnesses of love in the light of sins may not be new to those who remember the doctrine that Dante presents through the words of Virgil in the fourth circle of Purgatory, my theme will be the reciprocal one: how neurotic motivations constitute an obstacle for love. Namely, how these fundamental personality patterns that we recognise as basic characters (with traits that range from postures and motor functions to forms of thinking) manifest in terms of love. Therefore, with the experience I have gained as a professional psychotherapist, I propose in the following pages to deal with how love is impeded and falsified in each of the character neuroses and what the related problematic consequences are.

ENNEATYPE II: PASSION-LOVE

To enter fully into the actual theme of this chapter, it is appropriate to start the round of the characters with the second enneatype, since, as the proud are commonly considered among those who seem to be the most innocent of any sin, they are the ones who have the least trouble in being loving. In fact, they constitute the most "loving" character.

The fact that some characters are more or less "loving," however, is not due to their having a greater or lesser capacity to love in the deepest sense. We start from the premise that mental health—and the capacity to love that it entails—is interfered with by character pathologies of equal seriousness. It is natural for the seductive characters to appear more loving, since the falsification of love is in the foreground in them.

The fact that the proud do not appear to have any trouble in being loving does not mean that they do not have trouble with love. A diagnostic characteristic of the histrionic personality (the most aberrant form of pride) is its amorous instability, that is likewise bound to the instability and superficiality of the so manifest and intense emotions of this type.

Although I am sure that they arrive at the psychotherapist's with less pride than people with other characters (except for the lustful), the most common motive for which they turn to professional help is precisely that of problems with love.

How can this be so, given their loving disposition? Perhaps because of the high price their affection entails, a price that reveals their conditionality. While those with this seductive character go to a lot of trouble to offer a marvellous, unique, extraordinary love, their apparently reduced demands are also extraordinary, particularly with respect to love.

Neurotic needs are not satiated in the real world, because their passionate nature is a bottomless pit. Even in the ideal situation of meeting their true love, the proud may be sufficiently difficult so as to create a crisis in their relationship. They may be too invading, for instance, or too jealous, or very childish, irresponsible, or inconsistent. This is even more the case in the situation in which the neurotic needs and egoistic traits of the other appear alongside love. The proud always expect a bed of roses, and criticisms, impatience, annoyance, and other natural reactions of partners to their own defects will constitute not only wounds to their sensitivity, but also fundamentally wounds to their image, which is idealized, marvellous, always delightful and incomparable. These frustrations will naturally be factors of disinfatuation, and the passionate character of Enneatype II is little interested in a relationship without falling in love. Hence the characteristic pattern of a passionate search for love that goes from relationship to relationship—each time ending in disenchantment or boredom; enough for their unquenched yearning for love to seek a new object.

Not only the frustrations—consciously acknowledged or not—of daily life contribute to the deterioration of love relationships: what was so manifest in the life of the well-known historical lover, Giacomo Casanova, also comes into play. The actual story of his innumerable adventures informs us that it is not only disappointment in love that drove him to his adventures, but also the fact that he does not seek a life of love, but instead conquest for its own sake. Those who feed their pride with triumphs in love are not satisfied for long with the demonstration of the object of their interest finally yielding to them. Once this is achieved, they will become interested in reconfirming their attraction by broadening the scope of their conquests.

In both cases, however, these individuals suffer a type of underdevelopment of love. The relationship between the sexes constitutes such an intense passion that it can eclipse other interests in life, with the result that, in a certain sense, these people appear not to have a life of their own and put everything into their only vocation:

their family. This last situation would be fine if it were not for the fact that this apparent vocation harbors deep down a thirst for love that is excessively disguised as a form of givingness.

Naturally, none of this would be possible if it were not for the fact that needing-love in the proud person is in fact masked by giving-love. Self-deception is so perfect that these individuals are filled with their own giving (more than in the case of other characters). Regardless of what they may receive from others, their own giving (which entails "receiving" the need of the other) confirms their self-images as givers: the image of a great lover, of a great mother, or of a person with very delicate feelings.

Until now, I have spoken mainly of love between the sexes, which is the province of love in which Enneatype II tends to specialize and where they concentrate their form of giving and their masked need to receive. The mother-child relationship is also usually an important province, propitious for those who feed both their own givingness and the needs of others.

To summarize, however, let us review the particular imbalance in which the three loves that we considered at the beginning of the chapter express themselves in this character.

For a start, it is clear that they are relatively uninterested in love for God. Even beyond the love between the sexes, their orientation is more interpersonal than transpersonal. There is little room for "ideal objects" in this personality that so loves contact, for whom love is placed on the same level as the erotic and the emotional expression of tenderness. Their love life is made up of a combination of love for others and love for themselves—only that in this combination, as we have seen, the former masks the latter.

In my book *Ennea-type Structures*, I proposed the expression "egocentric generosity" for this phenomenon that is so central to EII (who seems to give all and receive nothing). Perhaps we could say that love for oneself is greater, while love for the other is its transformation—the result is an illusion by means of which one's own need is partly projected onto the other, and in part is simply negated or minimized, in so far as one emphasizes the giving of oneself. On a real scale, love for others would be situated in second place, between love for oneself and love for God, but it is the one that really attracts people's attention. So much so that, in many North American books circulating today about the enneagram of personality, this character is referred to as the *helper*. However, their incomparable capacity to pass their need off as disinterested large-heartedness is the first obstacle in their spiritual and therapeutic progress.

A cartoon in which an African woman can be seen with a Cupid that has to help her put an explorer into the cauldron vividly reveals the underlying egocentricity of seductive love, whether this manifests as a "vamp" or as a sweet, childlike character such as the one Dickens describes in his autobiographical novel, *David Copperfield*. Little Dora, by whom the writer is captivated on feeling the echo of his mother's character, only proclaims that she wants to help her adoring husband—but her incapacity to do so is manifest. In her desire to help him, she ends up devouring him just like the love of a vamp. In both cases, the other becomes a slave to a great anxiety for love that needs to be needed.

ENNEATYPE VII: PLEASURE-LOVE

We will continue our exposition with the seventh enneatype, since this is likewise a seductive, loving character. However, its way of seducing is somewhat different, as is its way of loving. The self-indulgent need an indulgent love above all, and as they prefer that no demands be made of them nor limits placed on them, they also offer the other permissiveness. So much so that La Bruyére, in his contemplation of human characters, highlighted one that seems determined to cultivate vices in others and to sing their praises.

If the ideal love that the proud seek as much as they offer is a passion-love, the ideal love of the glutton is somewhat softer, calmer, and problem-free. It is an agreeable love that seeks to please and which might be called a "gallant love," in association with court life at the time of Fragonard and the court of of Louis XIV. It is pertinent here to cite what Hipolito Taine says when comparing this form of love with that exalted by Boccaccio:

> Boccaccio takes pleasure seriously; passion in him, though physical, is vehement, even constant, often surrounded by tragic and rather mediocre events so as to entertain. Our fables are cheerful in a very different way. Man seeks entertainment in them, not enjoyment, he is joyful and not voluptuous, is sweet-toothed rather than a glutton. He takes love as a pastime, not as a rapture. It is a lovely fruit that he picks, savors and leaves.[4]

We may say that the psychology of EVII tends

4Hipolito Taine, *La Fontaine y sus fábulas,* (La Fontaine and his fables), Ed América Lee, Buenos Aires, 1946.

towards a confusion between love and pleasure—and hence between love and non-interference in the fulfilment of desires. But the expression pleasure-love does not fully evoke the phenomenon of this ever-so-light love of this friendly, jovial character who neither wishes to be a burden to others nor receive anything from anyone. We might well alternatively speak of a comfort-love, which invites us to evoke the agreeable, placid aspect of this form of love-life as well as its limitations.

We are provided with an illustration of the less-than-ideal expression of this comfortable love in the following joke from Rio de Janeiro, which seems appropriate to me in view of the sweet-toothed spirit of the city: a native woman is berating her husband, telling him that the maid is pregnant. The husband replies: "Ah, that's her problem." The wife insists: "But you got her pregnant!" He replies: "That's my problem." "And me, how do you think I appear in all this?" insists the wife. The husband replies lightheartedly: "That's your problem."

The fact that a pleasure seeker beats a retreat when faced with the person or situation that announces inconveniences, commitments, serious obligations, or restrictions is clearly one of the factors that makes gluttonous love an unstable, ever exploratory love. We know that all this increases as relations grow longer. But this is not the only factor, since the personality of the glutton is in itself curious and exploratory; the grass is always greener on the other side of the fence.

It is precisely the difficulty of satisfaction in the here and now of the real world that is the other important problem in the love life of "oral optimists," constantly pushing them towards the ideal, the imaginary, the future, or the remote. They think that it is desire that distances them from the present, but it is doubtful that this is any more than a subjective appearance: it is more an implicit dissatisfaction that motivates their continuous flight towards what is different. And it is difficult for the ideal of a totally indulgent sweetness that the glutton seeks to occur in real experience beyond the period of enchantment of a new relationship. Life has its problems, and in the physical world every calculation must be made taking friction into account. Pleasure-love seeks relationships without friction—and knows how to find them, though they can scarcely be called relationships. William Steig illustrates this eloquently in a drawing that, in spite of not referring to love per se, deals with the human condition (*The Steig Album*). A smiling man balances apples on his head and arms and suggests the type of person who is not only skilful but also derives a sense of mastery from interpersonal balancing acts.

There is a generalized friendly attitude in EVII. These are individuals who go to the restaurant and after a short while know the waiter or the cook. They also know the shopkeepers and make conversation easily. Their egalitarian attitude contributes to this and is part of their friendly, likeable, and seductive character. What is the basis for this? Camaraderie? There is an explorative aspect and, what is more, a search for novelty and experiences, a search for possibilites, for marketing, on the part of those who are always seeking to promote themselves. They remind one of the businessman who is searching for a market who, no matter whom he meets, wants to know the situation to see if there might exist an opportunity. The playful aspect also stands out: as they are playful, they approach others like a child does someone with whom he/she can play.

What underlies this non-relationship may be understood on the basis of the information that the Enneagram offers us about this enneatype: it is an enneatype (EVII) that is related to the antisocial characters (EVIII) as well as the self-absorbed, distant types (EV). The more the gluttonous tend towards the lustful, the more they go through life like Don Juans, in search of prey. No matter how gallant they may act, they carry inside themselves an opportunist as well as a schizoid, more interested in him or herself than in others. This form of egoism would be unacceptable for others were it not compensated by, at the least, an equal dose of gallant generosity.

Just as gluttons are generally specialists in making their desires acceptable to others, it is also true that in the specific terrain of love a person with this character tends to have little difficulty in getting his or her own way—even when this entails sacrifices and is unconventional, as in the case of infidelity. I recall a cartoon by Quino that presented a character with the typical physiognomic characteristics of a charlatan, sitting in his medical consulting room surrounded by diplomas. An old lady who has come to see him (presumably because of a heart complaint) is witness to the instructions that the young doctor gives to his secretary: "Call my wife and tell her to get in touch with my mistress to see how they can reach an agreement with my better half with respect to the children's party." In the next frame, we see that the old lady has fainted.

The discussion about the character traits of the narcissistic character in the DSM-III highlights entitlement, a sense of rights due to talent, due to superiority. However, the superiority that EVIIs pursue in a love relationship is different from that of people who go through life acting important and assuming a role of authority. In this case, we are dealing with a more subtle form of importance: they do not expect to be obeyed but to be listened to and acknowledged as someone in the know. The man may expect his wife to be his audience, for instance; likewise this occurs in a father with respect to his son. Correlative to the need of chatterboxes to be heard is naturally their not knowing how to listen, though they themselves may not be aware of this, since they offer great empathy in their attentive attitude. Also in questions of parenthood, the love of the self-indulgent is less than what it appears to be, due to their persuasive talent and charm. A father may hardly be present at home and still make himself loved, through presents and smiles, in such a way that his children are not aware until they are grown up of his absence. In this case, part of his love offering will be per-missiveness—only sometimes his children perceive it as his not wanting to make an effort, and they intuit that they would feel more loved if he set them limits.

Let us now see what the distribution of psychological energy is like among the three channels of love that we have distinguished in the charmers.

The hierarchy among these three loves is, in general, somewhat different from the case of the proud. While in the latter, love of the divine is practically eclipsed by love of self and love of the other, a religious orientation often appears in the gluttonous, and when this is not the case, one may observe a love of the ideal or an ideal love that corresponds to the sphere of love of the divine in the broadest sense in which I am inter-preting this term.

It is precisely religiosity or spiritual desires that may constitute an escape for people with this character. This entails not only neglecting the immediate and the possible for the remote and impossible, but also having difficulty in questions of discipline and a limited capacity to face the deep-seated discomfort of their own psyches. This often makes them amateurs who seek protection in spirituality without entering into a process of profound transformation.

With respect to love for oneself, the self-indulgence of EVII is more like that of an all too comfort-seeking, seductive father rather than that of a good friend to himself. But pleasure-love is naturally an attempt to compensate for a deeper sense of privation (as the movement between EV and EVII indicates in the Enneagram). One seeks pleasure precisely to flee from the psychological discomfort of anxiety and guilt, fleeing from these in proportion to the lack of affection towards oneself and to self-rejection.

Giving-love, as we have already implied, exists in this character, as it does in the previous one, in the form of seduction. It may be said, therefore, that it is present as strategic friendliness and availability. La Fontaine portrayed these well in his fables about the fox, who is always friendly towards the objects of his desire. We may also talk about an opportunistic-love. The title that a humorist gave to one of his books serves as an illustration of this: *To property via marriage.*

ENNEATYPE V: LACK OF AFFECTION

I said that there are characters that are apparently more loving than others, and I began with those that are so to the most marked degree. The one I shall comment on next is one of those that appear to be the least loving. Again, if love is an attribute of the essence of human beings—of their true self or central nucleus of being—it is something that is independent of character, which can be giving, available, or affirmative of others, or more distant, hard, or cruel. These are differences in programming or differences in interpersonal strategy and therefore belong to the world of pseudo-love more than to that of true love. However, the fact that schizoids seem less loving is valid both for those who experience this from the outside and for schizoids themselves. While hysteroids, the right wing of the Enneagram, find it easy to fool themselves with respect to their own capacity to love, it is more difficult for the more schizoid of the characters to fool themselves than anyone, and they may suffer acutely as a result of their incapacity truly to relate to others.

Although in their tendency to blame themselves the autistic are ignorant of the measure of spontaneous love contained in their psyches—from the viewpoint of the ideal of what they should be or do—it is also true that their programming turns against this impulse to merge with the other that Plato offers us in *The Symposium*, as a response to what love may be.

Schizoid characters are opposed to this impulse to merge with others since they harbor a true passion for avoiding ties. If love means being interested in others, "autistic" schizoids are the ones who are not interested. Not only do they hardly express their affections, but also they are cooler, more apathetic, more indifferent than others.

They like to receive, yes, but not to ask for things, because they have learned that asking may bother, and they are afraid that their voracity will lead them to an even greater frustration than the self-imposed frustration of being patient. Even their desire to receive love is dampened to the extent they have adapted to living with as little as possible, minimizing any need that entails dependence on others and needing to give in order to receive. Moreover, they find it difficult to know what they receive, as emotionally and implicitly they do not believe in love any more than EVIII, and they tend to think that those who manifest love do so out of their own conscious or unconscious interests. Or they do not believe themselves to be worthy of receiving love because they do not feel of enough worth or because their own disinterest in others leads them to feel that they do not give enough.

There is, therefore, a non-commitment to love, non-commitment to others, non-commitment to life, and over-control of the fear of commitment, of the threat that the needs of others entail. In their excessive intolerance with respect to the demands and expectations of others, they experience the desires of others mainly as limitations.

The most underdeveloped form of love is naturally the maternal, giving, and compassionate type of love; love of others is eclipsed by the love of ideals and preoccupation with oneself. There is scant feeling of camaraderie, little sense of community or fraternity with other mortals. These characters are also available very little to their children, whom they see—more so than in the case of other characters—as a weight, an impediment. On other occasions, however, there is a very intense projection of their own abandoned "inner child" onto their child, and this leads to overprotection and attachment to the child that is expressed in the form of a highly limiting relationship for the child.

Although they are egoistic, the avaricious are likewise so with themselves. They do not give themselves satisfactions; they push themselves and feel that they must carry out worthy deeds to give life a meaning.

In partner love, problems derive from their lack of availability, from their demand not to be subject to demands, from their isolation and scant empathy. Coexistence and matrimonial decisions—which entail a loss of privacy and of exclusive control over their own lives—are difficult. Sexuality may not be intense and may be perceived as another demand.

Love for God, whose demands are less patently present that those of their fellow man, become to a certain extent a substitute for human love, though this same love for God weakens if it does not rest on a sufficient experience of human love and love for oneself. However, it is easier and less conflictive to relate to an ideal object. Correspondingly, admiration-love (love of a child for its father or mother) is more developed in this character than generosity.

ENNEATYPE IV: SICKNESS-LOVE

In his book *The Seven Faces of Love,*[5] André Maurois coins the term "sickness-love" to designate the tormented love passion that characterizes the psychological world of Proust. Maurois says that, in contrast with Madame de Lafayette, Rousseau, or Stendhal, Proust no longer believes that the violence of passions "becomes legitimate as a result of the exceptional quality of the beings who are the object of these." And goes on to say: "We shall see that he considers passion-love to be an inevitable, painful, and fortuitous sickness."

Summing up this observation in the light of the

---

[5]André Maurois, *Cinq visages de l'amour,* Neuchâtel, Messeiller, 1942.

psychology of enneatypes, I would say that the love of both EII and EIV are passionate, the difference being that the proud believe in, exalt, and idealize their passion, while the envious (those who do not believe in themselves) suffer it.

We could say that the envious person is addicted to love. Envy is a feeling of lacking, a voracity for the other, a type of amorous cannibalism that is self-frustrating due to its own excess. Excess leads to frustration for two reasons: because it asks for more than can be expected, and because it bothers the other due to harrassment. The situation may be compared to that of a baby who bites its mother's breast as a result of its thirst; to the frustration that has led the baby to bite in the first place is added that produced by a mother who is hurt and makes a face or moves the child away.

Excessive demand is a response to a previous frustration, naturally. It is as if the individual were saying: "Give me, because you haven't given me enough, make it up to me." There is a connotation of revenge in this demand for compensation. The situation gets complicated for adults who are not complete strangers to themselves, because they know that they are "biters," and those who have a dark image of themselves—who perceive the aggressive charge that exists in their love—do not feel worthy and anticipate rejection. It is well known that anticipating rejection makes it come true. A well known joke explains this: someone goes round to a friend's place to ask if he can borrow the friend's guitar. On the way there, as he approaches the house, it occurs to him that it is a bad time to visit, since his friend might be having lunch. A few minutes later, still on the way there, he imagines that not only will he bother his friend, but that his friend will not be very willing to lend him his guitar. A guitar is a very personal thing for someone who spends so much of his time playing it. He knocks on the door and when his friend opens it with a smile and asks after the motive of his visit, the other person can do no more than reply: "You and your guitar can go to hell!"

Although envy expresses itself as an excessive asking for things, over-demandingness, this need for another person's love is based on a corresponding inability to appreciate or love oneself. These people depend excessively on the other not because of simple disconnection—as in the case of EIII—from their values, but as a result of a more present sense of undervaluing themselves that reaches extremes of conscious self-aggression or of self hate, a feeling of being ridiculous. When we speak of amorous passion, it is this type of love that is under consideration; sickness-love, as Maurois calls it.

We may say that the intensity of the importance that is given to love converts it into a great passion; but more than a passion, it might be called an illness, due to its element of dependence and insatiability. An additional difficulty blocking those who need affection so much from feeling loved, beyond their self-invalidation, is the invalidation of the other due to the feeling that: "If you love me, and I'm worthless, what kind of person are you? If I can deceive you so much, your need must be as great as mine." These people cannot conceive that they can be loved and do not allow themselves this satisfaction even when it might be said that they have achieved it. This is difficult, however, as a major feature of this type of character is seeing what is lacking instead of what there is. Love is not perfect enough or exalted enough or romantic enough to sate their sensitivity. A love that is so susceptible to being hurt or frustrated is contaminated by resentment precisely because of frustration or need.

EIVs are overly obliging characters, always available, accommodating, even obsequious, empathic, helpful, sacrificing. They support frustration and suffering even to masochistic levels, but at the same time charge or compensate for all their sacrifices through the exaltation of their own frustrated desire, which in turn becomes unconscious voracity.

Not only does the love of the envious become morbid as a result of the intensity of their thirst for the other, of their pessimistic interpretation of situations and their tendency towards self-frustration, but they also characteristically tend to ask for things by "getting sick." The association of the romantic attitude with sickness is well enough known for anyone to find this joke, that I came across some time ago in a magazine, funny: a doctor, leaning over the bed of a sick patient, says to the patient's mother: "Your son is a very sick poet."

The less permitted asking for things is and the more embarrassing desire is, the greater the need to "innocently" attract the object of desire, i.e., without guilt, through the intensification of the experience—histrionic intensification, we might say—of need and of frustration. The more forbidden the demand, the more this character needs to demand attention and care, apparently without intending to do so, whether through suffering, the role of the victim, or through physical symptoms and varying difficulties.

This is sometimes called "emotional blackmail" and is seen to exist not only between lovers, but also between parents and children. Seduction with weakness and need is as well known a feminine resource as the seduction of the irresistible, which expressed itself a few generations ago as fainting. It is, however, no more than the amplification of the cry with which every child calls its mother, asking for the satisfaction of its needs or for help.

However, there is a need to distinguish the lament of true compassion for oneself. In spite of their search for compassion and their complaints about not finding it, EIVs have trouble feeling this compassion for themselves, and do not even find it easy to receive. They do not even feel they have the right to receive good things, since not only do they not love themselves, but also they hate, undervalue, and reject themselves.

Transpersonal love for EIV, which goes beyond I and you, may be said not to be characteristically situated in the sphere of religiousness or in the sphere of goodness, but rather in the sphere of beauty. The higher values this person connects with are principally love for art and love for nature. Perhaps the love for a personal god gets mixed up with not feeling worthy, because the evocation of the divine only intensifies the pain of guilt. On the other hand, admiring is a very problematic thing for the competitive.

These characters may vehemently pursue eroticism, since it is something that takes the individual outside of the ordinary and quenches his or her thirst for intensity. But they have trouble giving themselves over to pleasure, not to the other; so much so that Wilhelm Reich interpreted masochism as an expression of an inhibition of the orgasm. The expression of giving-love is also prominent, of the *agape* type, which is manifested as orientation towards service, defense of the oppressed, and empathy. Those in need of pity do not know how to receive it, but easily take pity on others.

ENNEATYPE VIII: DOMINEERING-LOVE

To continue with the same order of characters as in the previous chapter, and dealing now with the upper zone of the Enneagram, let us examine the disturbance of love in the lustful.

If emotional indifference constitutes *an unlove*, it would be appropriate to speak of lustful *attraction* rather than lustful *love* as a *counter-love*. As a result of the thirst for intensity, the impulse of sexual union replaces rather than creates a vehicle for intimate union between people, in so far as the lustful (as Stendhal says of Don Juan) consider the opposite sex to be an enemy and only seek victories. "Don Juanish love"—Maurois reflects—"is like the taste for game. It is a necessity for activity that must necessarily be awakened by diverse objects."

Lustful love is a love like the prototype of the original "Don Juan" (that is, the seducer) who puts his desire before the other: a love that invades, uses, abuses, exploits, which at the same time demands a love that is confirmed via submission and allowing oneself to be exploited. He finds it difficult to receive because he does not believe in what he receives. Because, in his cynical position, he does not believe in the love of the other, he has to put it to the test. He tests the love of the other, for instance, by throwing him or her off balance and observing him or her in situations of emergency, or asking the impossible, asking for pain and indulgence as a demonstration of the other's sincerity.

Apart from the excessively domineering aspect of lustful love, there is a certain parallelism of intimate dissociation that derives from this character's great need for autonomy. Since these are tough types who are at war with the world, it is naturally difficult to speak of love in the sense of union or relationship—except in the outer sense. They receive the love of others badly, in as much as this constitutes a defense of their own independence. They reject what they are given and deny the desire per se to receive it, since this means an invasion of their system and entails the danger of feeling weak.

The partner love of EVIII is not only invasive, excessive, and domineering, but also violent. This could hardly be otherwise, since a violent character is revealed above all in private. Apart from being punitive, demanding, and provoking, these types are antisentimental: they seek a concrete, non-emotional, contact-love that lasts as long as the contact; a here and now love, without commitments and with rejection of dependence, which situates the person in relation to his or her fragility, his or her insecurity.

The pseudo-amorous aspect lies in the erotic; as well as in a seduction that is like a "purchasing" of the other or indulgence in certain situations. Compassion-love is rejected because it is incompatible with the marked emphasis of needing-love. Admiring-love, however, is more present; no matter how competitive these people may be, they are able to acknowledge and admire intensely, above all in the case of strong models. Love for self, however, is the strongest; love for others takes second place, despite their being apparently antisocial beings. They are contrary to norms more than to people in particular, and there is not so much difference as might appear between Enneatypes I and VIII as far as impulses are concerned. On the one hand, aggression is highly rationalized and is perceived as serving just causes (EI); on the other, aggression is recognized as such, and a kind of reversal of values exists by means of which good is considered bad and vice versa (EVIII). But there are human ties that go beyond what would be done in the name of what is supposed to be good, and social solidarity may lead to attitudes of revenge, of calls for justice for others, comparable to taking justice into one's own hands when it is a question of one's own life. Love for God or for the ideal and transpersonal is the weakest of the three.

When closely observed, the apparent love for oneself of the lustful can be seen as a pseudo-love. In the domineering insatiability of the search for pleasure, the person recognizes his or her own deepest need: hunger for love itself. It is not the inner suckling child that is satisfied, but a titanic adolescent who has set the goal of obtaining what was given him or her at the time, such that his or her own force on claiming it becomes a substitute for amorous desire.

ENNEATYPE I: SUPERIOR-LOVE

It is hard to distinguish between the habitual use of anger and hate, since the opposite of love is called hate. Accordingly, the passion of EI would be an anti-love. Its manifest character, however, is not the "counter-love" we described as characteristic of the violence, abuse, and exploitation of EVIII. We have already seen how EI is a good character—in the sense of someone who does not hate, but professes love instead.

Whereas the love of EII is an emotional phenomenon that lacks action, the love of EI is made up of intentions and acts that lack emotion. It is a barely affectionate love, it might even be said to be tough if the prohibition of toughness together with a conscious effort to be tender did not make this less apparent.

The personalities of Enneatypes VIII and I are comparably aggressive, except that in one, (valued) aggression is bare, and in the other (unvalued) aggression is negated and to a certain extent overcompensated, specifically in their love lives and in the loving aspect of human relations and situations. While EVIIIs are "bad" exploiters who demand indulgence or complicity, EIs face others as givers, generous types, by virtue of which they feel in possession of the corresponding rights.

Their aggression does not disappear, however, but metamorphoses into demands and superiority, into dominance and control over others similar to that of the domineering character—except that here it is disguised (in the eyes of the subjects themselves) as something that is justified by impersonal reasons.

One of Quino's illustrations explains the profound self-deception of those with a passion for justice or perfectionists (to distinguish them from amoral, lustful avengers), who disguise their desire as presumably disinterested, just demands. Justice, commonly personified as a woman whose bandaged eyes distinguish neither between persons nor objects, is wearing a bandage over only one of her eyes (which comically recalls the stereotyped pirate's patch) while cutting a slice of ham with her powerful sword.

The image here of the ham seems implicity to contradict this disinterested desire of the Puritans, characterized by Canetti in the portrait of an incorruptible vestal whose mouth is exclusively dedicated to the service of words and is never corrupted by receiving anything as low as the food that common mortals live on.[6]

The way of affirming desires is hence their transformation into rights; and while the rights of the rebel are sustained by brute force, those of the virtuous rest on their superior morals. This transformation of "I want" into "you should" is alluded to by Quino in the rest of his cartoon, which portrays, alongside the potent, somewhat corpulent

---

[6] op. cit.

woman (who as a parody of Justice was cutting the ham), a judge on a high seat. A judge who, due to his height and the type of seat he is sitting on, as well as to the presence of a toy on the floor and his gesture of licking his lips as he eats, is the image of a child. As impotent as it is powerful is the arm of justice.

To allude to this disturbance of love as "superior love" implies an "inferiorizing love": the other, who apparently benefits so much from this character's benevolent acts, is deprived of moral quality or spiritual stature. He or she is "vilified" to a certain extent, at the same time as being controlled and subjected to demands.

The inferiorization of the other is done via criticism, which may be explicit criticism that is conscious of the other's performance, decisions, or attitudes ("you have done this or that wrong" or "I do not approve of this or that aspect of your life") or the less explicit criticism of not being satisfied with the manifestations of the other, which do not reach the ideal of perfectionist excellence.

Among the three loves, the most dominant one here is that of admiring-love: love for greatness, for the ideal. Love for others takes second place, because it is a love in the name of ideals, a love that adheres to duty, at the same time as being a love that is lacking in tenderness. And even more in second place is to be found love of self, which is unconscious and denied. Their morals do not allow these characters their "egoistic desires," just as they do not allow the desires of others. We may speak of an anti-life attitude in these characters, in view of the excessive repressive control of their own impulses, of the taboo of their instinctiveness and of that of others. Whether it be their overprotective love towards their children or their possessive love towards their partners, there is not only a loss of spontaneity in these people themselves, but also a relationship that takes spontaneity away from others, who find themselves enveloped in an invisible repressive field.

This exceptionally conditional love demands unattainable merits and loses spontaneity. It is unaware of its destructiveness; it assumes the parental role not to support, but to interfere with the inner child of the other.

ENNEATYPE IX: COMPLACENT-LOVE

In the case of EIX, we may consider theirs to be an indolent love, like that of someone who is not fully alive. A lukewarm, "half-alight" love, in which the person is not complete. The contrary of passion-love, this may be characterized as a phlegmatic love.

We may likewise say of this love that it is a distracted love. It is willing to give a lot on the action level, but lacks attention to the true needs of others. As a concrete example of this lack of attention to the true innerness of others, I recall what someone once remarked about her—otherwise prestigious—analyst: "She is like a nanny." Well-meaning care lacking in deep communication, empathy, and enthusiasm. EIXs are surely the ones who most often give to others what is referred to as a "Greek present": a costly present which the recipient neither knows what to do with nor where to put.

The maternal love of EIX may even be perceived as invasive. I know, for instance, someone who remembers feeling suffocated by her mother's breast. Whether this is a real memory or an extrapolation to the past of subsequent and even present experiences, its content is significant. The girl also felt suffocated by the heavy quilt on her bed, a memory in which she seems to have crystallized her feeling of upset over a mother who looked after her in a concrete sense, but by whom she did not feel sheltered in an intimate sense.

This is usually a love that does not listen, but rather imposes its compulsion for being motherly or its marital abnegation on the other. The situation has been comically expressed by Woody Allen in an image in his film *Everything You Always Wanted to Know about Sex...*: a large breast roams the countryside squirting out milk like a gas pump as it advances.

The role of a generous person almost supposes a second nature; the person's self-sacrifice is part of the personality structure rather than a conscious role. This is, however, a more unconsciously seductive love than in other characters in so far as these people started early on to feel the need to renounce their own interests in order to be acceptable. Maybe they were not sure of their family situation—like in the case of an adopted child—and had felt they did not deserve it, that they are not up to it, that they could lose their place. Or they are the seventh of ten brothers and sisters and, in order to be seen and heard, in order to stand out, have found no other way to do so than by not creating problems. In other words, their present to their parents is the negation of their need, of their frustration, of their complaints or demands.

In so far as adaptation to the desires and demands of others is done predominantly via behavior, the love of EIX is—as in the case of EI—an active love, and in its aberrant aspect may be characterized as self-sacrifice or kindness without the experience of love. Both in the relationship between the sexes and in motherhood, this is an institutionalized love, adjusted to a usual social role.

Neglect for or disinterest in the more intimate experience of others may be understood as revenge for their excessive deference towards others (on a concrete, practical level): "passive aggression." Other forms of the same thing are negligence, Freudian slips, oversights, and even automatic obedience when this proves destructive.

When we examine EIX's experience of love in terms of the triad of fundamental aspects of love, we see that love for others predominates, while love for oneself is felt to be the deepest prohibition. Love for God tends to be a less prominent experience than human love, though a strong religious tendency may sometimes suggest the opposite. The religious tendency of this type of person is usually the result of identification with the values of society and a love of ritual. This may be an active and at the same time pious person, though nonetheless despiritualized in as much as his or her relationship with the divine does not entail a disposition towards (or an interest in) the mystic experience.

It does appear, however, that in some people a love for artistic activity provides a bridge between materialism and spirituality: art is a doing, an activity (especially sculpture or painting, the product of which is concrete), while nonetheless at times a veiled vehicle for spiritual and emotional experience. It has caught my attention, while reviewing diverse biographies, that both politicians and artists are to be found among the different EIXs. It would appear that some are EIX "as such," and others are those who have found the counterweight to an excessively practical life in interiorizing artistic work.

There is a lot of the mother in EIX, as if the giver identified with the mother role. Although at one point there was a lack of deep love, and the person is resigned to not feeling it, it is, however, as if he wished to fill this lack with his own giving to others, projecting his need onto a third party. Renunciation is altruistic, and the need of the other becomes one's own; the other thus becomes a substitute for oneself, for one's being.

The indolent (and a sub-group of these in particular) do, however, allow themselves a special form of self-love, a particular form of loving themselves that is both a deviation and a perversion: comfort-love. No matter how much work goes into getting comfortable, it is a substitute for true love of self, compensating for a deeper frustration through comfort, non-conflict, and softness. Alcohol, tobacco, and eating are expressions of this comfort-love. In types like the gregarious Mr. Babbit, with his big cigar, these stimuli substitute for affection, which is unattainable.

The flaw in self-love in EIXs manifests itself in their ignorance of their own deep needs; the disconnection of their inner child; the loss of spontaneous playfulness, having grown up before their time; and, on many occasions, the taking on of responsibilities in a highly visible way.

ENNEATYPE III: NARCISSISTIC-LOVE

Whenever I ask myself what vain love is or is like, I evoke the scene in an old film about Henry VIII's wives in which one of his lovers bursts into a room in the palace at the same time as the executioner is about to cut off the head of her predecessor; she is there to ask him which dress he wants her to wear that night. The scene highlights the monstrous disconnection of a minimum bond of love towards her rival, absorbed as she is in her own pleasure. But it is not just a pleasure as such, but a highly de-eroticized product of eros: passion for her appearance.

The fact that vanity is a product of the degradation of love became particularly obvious to me in the dream of a woman with a vain character in which, in the midst of a great world war, she only wanted to be taken to buy a dress, clearly demonstrating that she was not interested in anything else that was happening. In this scene, one feels her to be like a little girl who loves herself and wishes to be loved for that distinction.

Such worry about one's image is commonly called "narcissism," and hence the love of the vain may be called a narcissistic love. However, the term "narcissistic" has been applied to diverse human types, and interest in clothes, cosmetics, and personal appearance is only one of the manifestations of the narcissism that is characteristic of Enneatype III. Also common is the image of oneself as a competent person, as someone who can do things, who has capabilities. Anticipating a little the theme of the final chapter (on the ills of society), I would say that the competitive desire for efficiency asphyxiates the person's capacity to love and makes the love of others irrelevant. A brief cartoon from Quino expresses this very well: in the first scene a businessman can be seen sitting in his office reading the passage from the Gospels that says that it will be easier for a camel to pass through the eye of a needle than for a rich man to enter the Kingdom of Heaven. In the next image, we see him calling the Museum of Natural History of Cairo to inquire as to the size of a camel. He then tells his secretary to call up Krupp Industries... We are narcissists when we sell our souls for glory—an entity that only exists in the eyes of others. It is paradoxical that what the world calls love of self (indulgence of one's own desire like the little girl who wants to be bought a dress) coexists with an inability to recognize one's own value. Self-appreciation becomes dependent on the appreciation of a spectator who approves, wants, and distinguishes—or more precisely—the world's appreciation becomes a palliative that distracts one from experiencing emptiness, artificiality, and loss of identity.

Working on one's image distracts from working on self, and while it constitutes a contrary position to what is natural and spontaneous, it entails a good capacity for control over one's acts. But excessive self-control sup-poses an obstacle to the capacity to love, which implies a non-capacity to surrender. The appreciation of control is so refined that it overshadows that of love, which may be felt to be something that is secondary to work and success, something sentimental, small, and in bad taste.

One complication is competing against one's partner; another, excessive control of one's partner or children; a third, difficulty in giving oneself, which may manifest on a physical level like in Jodorowsky's caricature. An elastic, sexual superman with infinite fingers that end in tongues, has an extraordinary capacity to give pleasure that absorbs him so much, however, that he has no atten-tion left for delight. Behind this incapacity to give one-self is distrust, fear of rejection, fear of falling into the void. An underlying despair in an apparently optimistic character, namely feeling that one has to maintain every-thing under control, to take care of oneself.

For those whose image demands self-control and control of situations, it may be that the desire for love is associated with a desire to allow themselves to be con-trolled, and rightfully so, since only by renouncing con-trol and manipulation can they allow themselves to be deeply touched. I recall having seen this theme dealt with in the film *Swept Away*, in which a woman develops an intense passion for her fellow survivor of a shipwreck after he dominates her. However, following the period in which love entails the sacrificing of vanity, this may be reinterpreted as mere masochism, and the same occurs when the sacrifice of one's image does not receive the corresponding desired love.

Narcissistic love is a false love, different from the car-ressing love of EII in as much as it expresses itself more in acts than in emotional expression. It is associated with an attitude that is effectively more obliging. EIII is, however, more affectionate than EI, whose benevolence is felt less. Faced with frustration, however, these types turn accusatorial, and adopt the stance of an aggressive victim. They do not protest, like EIV, since they hardly say what they feel, but rather use accusation to hurt the self-esteem of the person who has frustrated them. They express their anger without apparent scandal, with precise, sharp, cutting words—preferably in front of witnesses. It is at these moments, in these phases of the relationship, when the fact that they do not truly believe in love comes to the fore the most. Even when they receive love, they cannot believe in it, since might it not be the result of their seductive art and their appearance, of their capacity to dazzle and to hide their own defects? Doubt—though far from consciousness—feeds seduction, and the more these people give themselves over to cultivating their image, the more they find themselves at the mercy of others and the more they defend themselves from others via self-control and by cultivating their independence. Their independence is fed by the dependence of others: it is the power that confirms that they have become indispensable. The love of EIII therefore knows how to make itself indispensable and feeds dependence.

Plastic man and woman fool themselves, however, as they are ignorant of their inhumanity, and thus are able to maintain an illusion of benevolence. The loving role dominates, as all roles efficiently dominate. Ignorant of their feelings, it is easy for them to confuse the imagined feeling with reality. The same loving role may be difficult to sustain, given that the intensity of the passion to please entails intolerance of criticism when faced with the danger of frustration. The facets of the disturbance of love that then appear are coldness and aggression.

Love for others is submerged in self-image. It is, on the one hand, a love founded on the need for validation from the other. On the other hand, it is oriented towards serving the need of the other, which in turn supports the self-image That is, other people's needs are primary, and generosity is a seductive strategy.

In the world of relationships in general, it may be said that these types need others, because they feel via their recognition. They are more friendly than the majority, more extroverted, they go out of their way more for others. They radiate happiness, benevolence, and adaptability, though superficiality as well. Both on the social plane and that of sentimental relationships, we may speak of a seductive love, since they appear to be there more for others than they really are, and the way in which they make use of the other is hidden. A master portrait of this situation is the character of Becky in *Vanity Fair* by William M. Thackeray.[7]

Love of God in the vain character tends to be eclipsed by human love in its two forms: love for oneself and love for others. This characteristic trait has surely contributed to the secularization of North American culture and of the modern world in general. Common sense and utilitarianism predominate over universal values; people are admired, but the abstract or transpersonal are not appreciated. As far as a spiritual path is concerned, in general this is the kind of person who would say: "What path?" In short, a mundane person, as caricatured by Chaucer in the character of the elegant, practical monk in his *Canterbury Tales*.

---

[7]Editorial Planeta, Barcelona, 1985 (Spanish edition of the cited work).

ENNEATYPE VI:
SUBMISSIVE-LOVE AND PATERNALISTIC-LOVE

Our final topic is the disturbances of the love life of the fearful. To speak of fear is to speak of distrust, and an incompatibility exists between distrust and love—since to speak of distrust is to speak of feeling one is faced with a possible enemy, and it is not easy to love one's enemies.

They are feared, and as fear requires being on guard, giving of oneself is feared. There is fear of being tricked, subjugated, humiliated, controlled. This also leads to self-control and to the inhibition of the flow of life in view of an excessive need for protection.

No less important than all this, however, is the contamination of love-life with the authoritarian motivations that characterize this type of personality. I say "motivations," in the plural, so as to encompass within this term both the passion of giving orders and the more common passion of obedience—or, rather, of having an authority to follow.

Although I did not indicate in the presentation that I made of the characters the three varieties that *protoanalysis* distinguishes among each of these, it is necessary in the case of the authoritarian-suspicious types that make up our EVI to differentiate between those that are too inclined towards hero worship from those who tend towards grandiosity and a heroic view of themselves. In the former case, these are highly dependent people, for whom the anxiety of choosing and insecurity with respect to their own capacities lead them to an excessive need for the father; in the latter, we are dealing with those who, in rivalry with their own fathers (at times in a

144

mother's body) *assume* authority and elevate themselves with respect to others in expectation of their subordination. While the anxiety of the former is calmed by finding protectors, the latter are placated by feeling themselves to be powerful and obeyed—as can be seen in a caricature of Hitler. Standing before an immense crowd, surrounded by his chiefs of staff, in a stadium in which a huge swastika can be seen, he opens his speech by saying: "I think I may say without fear of being mistaken..."

It is interesting to know that Hitler, who was maltreated by his father when he was a child, developed the intention to give his country a good father. Extreme examples (such as the exaggeration of the caricature) help us to understand the greater subtleties, for the many who go through life offering themselves as fathers to those needy for authority. For one who likes giving orders, obedience is a declaration of love; to achieve obedient children, however, he will have to offer himself as a benevolent father, like the wolf in the fable dressed in sheep's clothing.

However, the role of the father is no more loving than the role of the son, and the majority of cowards spend their lives, just like little orphans, seeking the protection of someone stronger. Their position may be translated as an exchange of admiration and recognition: "Accept me as a son and I will give you filial devotion."

It is not that differences in mental as well as bodily stature do not exist, and it is not a question of it being right in a specific relationship that one or the other makes certain types of decisions; is it not equally certain that the majority of people are incapable of egalitarian, fraternal relationships? This is the disturbance of love that arises in response to fear, and is characteristic of those people in whose personality this is central. Just as some overplay the part of little orphans, seeking protec-

145

tion, there are others who are too "paternalistic." One seduces by means of inoffensiveness; the other by offering guidance and his or her knowledge of certain truths. We are hence talking about a father who says things the way they are, who is passionate about being a teacher, and who asks for agreement, faithfulness, and obedience not only in acts, but also in the way of seeing things.

Apart from a problem of distrust or excessive giving of oneself from a sense of obligation or fearful duty, there exists the problem of ambivalence. There is love and hate, trust and distrust, domination and at the same time submission—and a continual questioning about what the true feeling or right attitude is.

I think that when Freud defined maturing as a leaving behind of infantile ambivalence, he said something universally valid, though especially descriptive of the situation of EVI, for whom managing to love is a putting aside of the hate inherent in a situation of enmity towards a world of phantoms.

Apart from the presence of aggression in the ambivalent world of the fearful, love worsens their accusatorial character, which may turn into that of a torturer.

One cannot talk of love for oneself when one has the self-condemning position that is characteristic of the psyche of EVI. Love of the person's inner child is lacking in this psyche, which functions from the position of control—in the name of duty—more than from that of desire. It may be said that the fearful accusatorially demonize themselves: an inner demon points outside of itself saying "there is the devil," principally accusing spontaneity and the body. Everything has to pass through conscious control, as it is implicitly thought (in line with Freud) that one is monstrous deep down inside, and that one's unleashed "id" would be a horrible thing, incompatible with civilized life.

As far as partner relationships and the social world are concerned, fear and aggression appear in continual interchange. These people fear spontaneity as if it were aggression, and repression engenders true aggression. Surely the sum total of aggression in our world is partly a reflection of the great prominence of the EVI character in its bosom.

As regards the commandment to love God above all things, it would appear that EVIs are not as guilty as they are in their failing with respect to the other two loves. There is a religious tendency, an archetypal tendency, towards the ideal world, that sometimes becomes a substitute for valor in the world of action, as suggested in this Nasruddin story in which a tailor says he is going to have the suit ready by a certain date, "God willing." The customer replies: "And when would it be ready if we left God out of it?" Religiosity also substitutes for the interpersonal emotional aspect. Think of the love of so many Nazis for their mythology, their classics and great music, in an attitude according to which "my God is greater than your God, my culture is greater than yours" or "I am closer to greatness than you."

These people think themselves to be gods because of their proximity to their God, but in this there is something of the passion of conceit that is part of the paranoid system. The search for love is transformed into a desire for power, which in turn is a desire to identify with the powerful father figure. One of Canetti's characters illustrates this well, roaring, as if from Mount Sinai, with his great mane of hair.[8] He paternalistically wishes to confuse others (and is surely confused) into interpreting

---

[8]Elias Canetti, *Der Ohrenzeuge. Fünfzig Charaktere*, Carl Hanser Verlag, München 1979 (tr.: *Ear Witness: Fifty Characters*).

his passion to impose the truth according to the Book of Books as love for others. Love of ideologies or quasi-divine characters is felt as being close to love for God, but it is a kind of vicarious narcissism; like a child who says to another of the same age that "my daddy is bigger than your daddy, look how big my daddy is."

Although in general I do not consider myself an especially severe person, I often am severe in my therapeutic role and each time I speak or write about the enneagrams of personality. When, at the end of the Prologue to this book, I said that it had turned out severe, I was implicitly referring to this chapter. I hope that some of my readers have the "strong stomach" referred to in one of the North American reviews of my previous book dedicated to the psychology of the enneatypes.[9]

> It is a demolition, you writhe, you cry, but if you have a shred of honesty you cannot stop looking. His descriptions get too close to the intimate. There is abundant evidence; the facts pile up with abundant precision ... There is nowhere to run to and nowhere to hide: he is talking about you ... This is not a path for those who have a weak stomach. But who said that transformation might be easy?

---

[9]*Ennea-type Structures*, op. cit.

IV

The Ills of the World in the Light of the Enneagram

AN ENNEAGRAM OF SOCIETY

In the title I have used "ills of the world" and not "social pathologies" because I prefer the popular expression to the academic one. For my purposes, ordinary language has in this case a virtue that it does not share with technical jargon: although the word "ill" may initially evoke the meaning of "illness," it nonetheless still retains a moral signification.

To call social dysfunction an illness is to develop the view of society as an organism that characterizes the modern formulation of the science of systems. Just as, in general, systems with diverse levels are reflected in their constitutive elements and functions, we may agree that individual pathologies would have their corresponding social pathologies, and the "capital sins" of the individual correspond to certain basic ills of the organism of our species on the Earth. And if at an individual level mental illness may be defined as a condition that hinders the realization of a person's potential, we may also define the fundamental ills of the world as social phenomena that constitute basic forms of interference with the potential of humanity.

More than eight thousand human problems have been listed in the *Encyclopedia of World Problems and Human Potential*.[1] Among these diverse problems, present day futurologists seek a central nucleus, in an attempt to discern a metaproblem—a unitary problem set underlying its multiple, interrelated manifestations. Between these two levels—the thousands of specific problems and the central problem—is to be found the level of analysis I propose, which is an invitation to consider nine capital or basic aberrations of society through "civilized" life.

It is obvious that resonances may be found between collective processes and institutions and psychological processes on an individual scale; so much so that at one time it was popular to study the specialty of "culture and personality." To this category belongs the formulation that I shall explain below concerning social aberrations in the light of the Enneagram. Sociologists have protested about "psychologistic" interpretations that propose individual causation of what is social without paying sufficient attention to the causal social factors acting on the individual psyche. Obviously a circular relationship exists between the levels of organization, even though these are different levels in a hierarchy that goes from the

---

[1] Edited by the Union of International Associations, K. G. Saur, Munich, New York, London, Paris 1986.

elemental to the complex. Aside from all this, the isomorphism or parallelism between the patterns that may be recognized at one or the other level is also clear, such that we intuitively comprehend the relevance of the diverse experiences of "sick love" with respect to social metaproblems. Through the formulation of these metaproblems, I shall be developing what may be called an Enneagram of Society.

AUTHORITARIANISM

I shall start with the central triangle of the Enneagram, which on the individual psychological plane corresponds to cowardice. Fear is a universal emotion, but when it dominates an individual's character it is associated with an excessively hierarchic world view. Fear has a lot to do with authority, because we were originally tormented by those giants that surrounded us when we were little: our parents. Above all, the father figure is the symbol—if not the executor—of authority in the majority of homes. For this reason, fear contributes to a person's tendency towards superiority/inferiority relationships. Fear is therefore a passion that leads in the social world to the existence of the bossy and the bossed.

Just as a person who has a distrusting character experiences in an especially acute way the struggle within him or herself between the tyrant and the slave, the accuser and the accused, the persecutor and the persecuted, the blamer and the blamed, we also function in this way within society. It is easy to understand that the prevalence of a character prone to intimidation is favorable to the establishment of an authoritarian hierarchy. And vice versa, it may be thought that an authoritarian society favors the development of the fearful character. The most authoritarian hierarchy in our present day society, which appeals above all to this type of character, is naturally the army; in past times the Church was more authoritarian than today. (There were times, now almost forgotten, when the Church was much more powerful than the empire, and the most powerful man in the Western world was the Pope.)

Such a hierarchic view means that the person is oversubjected to authority, and when there exists an overtendency to surrender one's own authority (or, to put it another way, an *under*capacity to be an authority for oneself), an overtendency towards obedience, overemphasis on a child's programming to depend on a strong father, this means that entire peoples are found to be especially eager to exalt and follow someone with the passion to command.

The most notorious case was naturally that of Nazi Germany. EVI predominated in the German people, and particularly this fearful, orderly character, with a strong sense of duty, both idealistic and an idealizer of authority, in which the individual fears making a mistake and at the same time longs for certainties. This type of character wants to be talked to in a certain manner so that he or she may feel that the speaker knows, the speaker is right. We know that the typical discourse of fanatics is like this. The Nazi people was curiously enough a caricature of the Jewish people, in so far as the notion of the chosen people was taken by the Germans from their enviously hated enemies. There are many films that reflect the Nazi world and so much has been written about it, that it is as if we were still digesting it; as if we still had a lesson to learn, a lesson that seemed to have been learned a few decades ago and which allowed us to leave authoritarianism to one side. We felt that we were already prepared not to fall once more into the aberrations of nationalism, but it seems not to be so. To the contrary, authoritarianism is reaffirming itself in the world, and nationalisms are vying for power everywhere.

Although there is a huge gap between the prophetic faith of those who felt destined for a role of salvation—through sacrifice in the name of their ideals—and aggressive nationalism, for which the exaltation of patriotic or national values constitutes the premise of a right, I think that fear has been the central structure not only of the German people in contemporary Europe, but also of Western Christian culture and of ancient Jewish culture. Nietzsche, the great critic of Christian culture, said that our morality is a morality of slaves—a morality of the oppressed that allows us to endure oppression. We do not value courage like the ancient Greeks; we value humility, obedience, "behaving well," because this is what the authorities want.

The social pathology I am discussing is what is technically called "authoritarianism." Authoritarianism manifests in the individual in a series of characteristics such as submission to those above and aggression towards those below (the so often cited "pecking order"). In human hierarchies, aggression is received from those further above and resentment is unloaded on those below or on those outside the group itself, on a "scapegoat."

I once saw a cartoon of someone watching a program on television in which Fidel Castro is lecturing the masses; the viewer changes channels and Mao appears haranguing the masses; finally, he switches off the television and begins aggressively to harangue his dog. The same is repeated down through the generations: authority is abused with one's children and in this way the authoritarian character is perpetuated.

This is the most visible aspect of authoritarianism—ordering and being ordered, alienation of one's own power, giving too much power over to others, dependence on pseudo-parental figures (such as the "boss" who acts *in loco parentis*), seeking protection in the benevolence that is conceded by and is expected from a parent, and putting on an act of benevolence so as to be able to exploit and control even better. Many people have thought that the institution of the State would not exist if it were not supported by this microscopic form of government that is the patriarchal organization of the family. The most internal aspect of the relationship of authority is the use of accusation, the placing of blame. We know that throughout history people have been kept in their place by threatening them with hell. "What kind of person are you? A father does not speak like that!"; "What treason towards the fatherland!" ... And all accusations are based on an ideology.

It is apparently true that ideologies are dying, they are in their death throes. Many people have reported this. Marx was perhaps the first to point this out, showing how ideologies are an instrument of manipulation, and since then there have been many others: Orwell, Manheim, Marcuse... But although it is an aberration that nowadays it is difficult to find someone who believes in something, an ideology exists that we implicitly share: *that the system functions and that it is legitimate.* For instance, it would occur to very few people to assume that the sovereign States, namely governments, are questionable and that there might be a better form of coexistence. Some time ago, it was forbidden to be Marxist just because Marx had questioned the need for and the goodness of the State. The best of Marx was precisely this questioning; his true legacy consists in the beginning of the search for alternatives and not in the solutions he offered. He is similar in this sense to Freud, who, by pointing out certain things that functioned poorly, had a profound effect on our cultural history, even though his proposal is now highly revised and few orthodox Freudians remain in our day and age.

The implicit ideology that everything is relatively all right and that things are being done the best they can be ignores the fact that there is an invisible power structure, as well as enough people interested in things *not* changing. We feel ourselves to be part of a democratic world, but the Greeks were much more so than we are. Although slavery existed, *each citizen* was paid to attend the *agora*, and it was a duty to participate in the discussions. Decisions were taken by the "government of the people by the people," with the implicit belief that everything was self-regulating. We now live the fiction (and it is an ideology) that we are free because we can choose between one candidate and another, an act that often turns out to be irrelevant.

Naturally, the current situation cannot be compared with the times of Galileo, when the Church ordered what we were to believe. With this I wish only to illustrate that command is not so much a question of brute force, but above all authority per se. An entire art exists in assuming authority, an art in appearing that one is legitimate and in appealing to the principles that allow us to appear so. An art, also, of making others feel like children so that they take us for wise, kindhearted parents.

With all of the above, I have attempted to explain the social pathology known as authoritarianism, whose prototypical institution is the State.

MERCANTILISM

Let us now go to the opposite point at the base of the triangle, point III, which in the individual character is related to vanity, glory, shining, and appearances, and which leads a person to become vividly interested in competing and coming out on top. On a social plane, it is obvious that we live in a world of intense competition—in a "rat race"—hurriedly racing faster and faster in pursuit of something. Think of the world of industries, of corporations, of business. The system is built in such a way that those who do not run at the same speed as the rest do not survive. Competitiveness, given this form of system, is intrinsic to its functioning, and as a result, we have no time for anything: no time to live, but only time to run in pursuit of something; we have no time to grow, to breathe, to nourish ourselves.

Allegedly we have experienced thousands of years of progress. However, some time ago I was reading the reflections of a well-informed anthropologist who said that the majority of primitive tribes dedicated some three hours a day to survival activities. We have the idea that primitive people led a very hard life, because they had to hunt, thus risking their lives constantly, while our life is privileged, with our stores and that great invention, money. But with the three hours a day that they dedicated to hunting they were much better off than many people in current day society who carry out activities with no personal meaning during eight hours sitting at a desk, or cleaning windows, sealing bottles... in an environment that is incomparably less healthy and less beautiful.

The world is characterized by this race towards success, not only on an individual level, but also at the level of the social success of certain groups. But there is another aspect of the vain personality that has also turned pathological: living for fictitious values, which are alien to life. Obviously, many values are intrinsic. Breathing is valuable not because one has been told that it is valuable to do so; if one breathes with attention, this activity can be a delight. Likewise, it is not necessary to demonstrate the value of eating to anyone. Aesthetic values, true cultural values, are not values because one wants to show to others that one knows something: they constitute a subtle food. But, are these the values that we live for?

There are people who live mainly for borrowed values, such as Molière's *Bourgeois Gentilhomme*. Led by the desire to be as others wish them to be, they go to great pains to have what others have, to dress and think according to the latest fashion. This affects the motivation for profit, as Veblen has so well observed when speaking of "conspicuous consumption" (i.e. wealth that is part of an exhibition of triumph). Moreover, the value of something in the market is fictitious with respect to its use value. Whatever our personality, it is a fact of contemporary life that the market devours us, and love of money—like cancer—competes with love for others, for ourselves, and for the highest values.

We are talking about mercantilism, which we certainly have to consider among the capital ills of the world. In his latest book, Quino explains what this is very well, without the use of words: a very important monument can be seen in a public square. There is a lock, a giant lock—like that of any door—in a high column on top of a high pedestal. Surrounding the monument, as if paying homage to their heroes, are to be seen the representatives of all the hotel firms. The boss appears, the manager, and even the maid with the vacuum cleaner. It could have had to do with anything else other than a hotel, but what is the meaning of all this? That in our present world, it is what sells that is worshipped. Values are perverted. We live overdistracted from love for art, love for God, love for intrinsically real things, love for people, for ourselves, for the family.

"Mr. Money is a powerful gent," who has hired us and has taken over our energies.

THE INERTIA OF THE STATUS QUO

Having seen two of the ills of society, authoritarianism and mercantilism, what would be the third cornerstone of social dysfunction, according to this application of the Enneagram to the problems of our collective life?

I said that on the individual plane the upper vertex of the triangle may be conceived as a tendency towards automatization, mechanization, disconnection, towards walking the world like a robot, converting man into a creature of habits. Life is not lived creatively, life is not lived in the strictest sense of the word, but rather one goes with the flow and succumbs to an inner stupor.

Who does not consider him or herself to be inwardly benumbed? I think that this is one of the most universally shared ills of the world, but there also exists a characterological question: there are people who are not so badly off in other senses as in this particular sense of being too inert, ingratiated, comfortable, blind.

On the social plane, this corresponds to the status quo; on the individual plane, we find ourselves faced with an unmovable quality, as if by becoming robot-like, human beings lose their evolutionary capacity. But society also loses its capacity to evolve. We are overinstitutionalized, and it is a characteristic of all institutions to become fossilized. When an institution is fresh and new, it exerts its function. By the second generation, after some years have passed, it starts to do things in an automatic way, disconnected from its first aims. And a moment comes when it turns into a pure institution. No one moves anything, but a paralyzing power is felt, a retarding factor.

Education may serve as an example. It would appear that institutional education in the world has good intentions. Much thought is put into it, numerous meetings are held, how reforms could be carried out is discussed, large sums of money are invested.... But almost all those involved in this enterprise are "burnt out" or demoralized. They feel that nothing happens, that they cannot do anything real, since institutional inertia is so powerful. Although this might be considered rather innocent with respect to other ills of the world, it is not, since it is a question no more and no less than of the *organ of development:* the institution which is fundamentally responsible for development. To educate is to further the development of individuals. And this process fails categorically when it does not fulfill this function, in so far as it is occupied with something completely different: the heart is not educated, people are not educated to live, they are not guided towards being themselves, the spirit—what we are—is not developed. And no one questions this. If one begins to talk about this theme, one can appreciate how education has been converted into a great white elephant, an unmovable institution. Why? Because it is immense and it is highly bureaucratized.

What sovereign governments are with respect to

authoritarianism, and what corporations (especially multinationals, which now have more power than governments, since governments cannot go very far without money) are with respect to mercantilism, bureaucracy is with respect to the power of inertia. We know, for example, that all tyrannies surround themselves with large bureaucracies that contribute to stabilizing them.

But it is not that bureaucracy, the market, or government are intrinsically dysfunctional, but rather that they externally crystallize real pathologies: *overgovernment, overcommercialization, overorganization.* They say that when God made the world, and He saw that it was good, the Devil came along and told Him: "Hey, why don't we institutionalize it?"

The instrument that becomes the end turns into a deadweight, as occurs with certain machines in works of science fiction. This theme of the machine that escapes from human control has been widely exploited, and justly so, since we feel that the world is getting out of hand. We should be considering overpopulation as the number one problem of today's world. All other problems—justice, inequality, violence—are getting worse because we do not all fit on the surface of the planet. The progression increases day to day, and in most parts of the world there is no one to put a brake on it. Perhaps nothing reveals in such a paradigmatic way how the overorganized, overrationalized, and overgoverned world that we have created is something that is escaping from our control. I think that if we had control over ourselves, this would surely be reflected in our social life and we might aspire to a more voluntary collective coexistence.

REPRESSION

These three ills that I have pointed out—authoritarianism, mercantilism, and excessive conformity—explain many things. But let us examine others. On the plane of individual problems, point I of the Enneagram—to the right of the upper vertex of the triangle—represents that facet of our neurosis that we may call "perfectionism," which affects all of the characters to a greater or lesser extent. We demand that we be a certain way, in spite of our rebelling against our own demands. We lack a certain self-acceptance, and we do not allow ourselves to be natural or spontaneous. We live disconnected from our inner nature and its wisdom.

I referred previously to the oligarchic character described by Theophrastus, who has many political implications. Theophrastus caricatured him as saying to a colleague: "Look, we, who know better, must control the affairs of the people." This expresses a *superior* position in life, and this is a character that is not only superior, but "inferiorizing"—a highly moral character who, from his or her moral superiority, judges others as immoral, degenerate, and perhaps worthy of being sent to jail; or who assumes the right to "educate" them and, if they do not let themselves be educated, possibly decides that they have to be bashed on the head with a civilizing mace. We have a good example in the crusaders (and their adversaries), who insisted on educating the unbelievers or infidels, on converting them to the true religion. "Praise be to God and give them the mace," as we might paraphrase the Spanish refrain (*A Dios rogando y con el mazo dando*); aggression in the name of religion, as in so many wars.

This is an inseparable facet of civilization. When we say that we are "civilized" people, we mean that we are people of a certain dignity, a certain cultural refinement, a certain psychological or spiritual evolution, a certain quality. We think that we are civilized and not barbarian, not primitive. But is that so? Up until now, civilized man has shown himself to be the most destructive of animals. And if we do not realize this, it is because we idealize ourselves and reinterpret our will for power as meritorious privilege, as in the case of the oligarchic or aristocratic character.

Clearly, the aristocratic character has fulfilled a function in crystallizing the patrician classes, the privileges of the nobility, and the projection onto the world of inferiorizing relationships, giving rise to injustice in the name of justice. It is not just a question of privileges: these privileges are protected by *repression*.

When the word repression is used in the social sense, its meaning is different from the psychological sense. Psychoanalysis calls not wanting to *see* certain things repression, but when we are talking about a repressive or prohibitory culture or society, we are referring to the fact that "those who know," the moral, the good, tell others what to do and what not to do. In relation to this, here is another anecdote: some time ago I found in a bookshop in Madrid a thick tome on "cultures that repressed humanity" written by a professor in law from the University of Zaragoza, Spain. I bought it, thinking: "Let me see what he has written, which cultures he calls repressive." The book starts with primitive cultures, continues with the Egyptian and Babylonian cultures, and then every other one we know... not one is left out! The fact is, they are all repressive. Repression is an organ of society and our evolution, the evolution of an illness.

The exaggeration of what is repressive may be seen in the enormous hypertrophy of the criminalizing judicial and police system of modern governments. Today in the United States, the "prison crisis" is becoming obvious. There are so many people in prisons that the public budget cannot cover the cost, and what is more, people recognize that the system is not of any service at all to the majority. If what we pursue is that people change and improve, we will have to consider it much more likely that this occurs by being in contact with the good people there are outside. Prison, we know, is more a "breeding ground" for delinquency. Prisons concentrate the people with the most problems, and so the situation of deterioration increases at an extraordinary speed.

The only justification for prisons is to protect society from certain highly dangerous people, but the majority of those that are there are not so. So many of the people who are in prison in the United States got into the artificial paradises of drugs, and they have committed no greater crime than that of buying a little marijuana, for instance. For a culture like that of the United States, this is an important crime, because "what might this lead to" if it were allowed? "You start off with marijuana and you are sure to end up cutting your mother up into little pieces ... you don't know what might happen in an altered state of consciousness." The fear of a lack of control is a very North American phenomenon, but it also forms part of Western society, with a notably anti-Dionysian culture, with very little capacity for surrender. Although the Christian symbol of wine wishes to remind us of a kind of *extasis* that surrender to a higher power produces, a culture that is saturated with prohibitions and demands can hardly promote the capacity for surrender.

The overcontrolling and overpolicing aspect of society is self-perpetuating. The more something is criminalized and the more it is said that "you are bad," the more "bad" will be done, resulting in greater problems for society. Our hypersocial society, which weighs too much on the person with its "you have to do what I tell you to do," "you have to be a good citizen," "you have to be patriotic," generates rebellion and criminality.

VIOLENCE AND EXPLOITATION

The antisocial character is only the most extreme form of a much more common character that we could simply call the rebel. We have already spoken of the lustful: intense, violent people, who do not support frustration, who demand immediate satisfaction. These are people who believe in attaining things and in taking justice into their own hands, in personal revenge rather than delegating to institutions.

This punitive character becomes very obvious at a collective level when we think of Mexican culture, with its *machismo* and its firearms. Mexico inherited this aspect twofold: from Moctezuma and from Hernán Cortés, from the bloodthirsty Aztecs and from the *conquistadores* who rode roughshod over them. This character that is so strong, so extreme, so intense, expresses itself in two ways in the world. One is an antisocial expression per se, that would appear not to be an "ill of society," but rather the attribute of antisociety: criminality. I would say that this declared or explicit criminal violence is a relatively lesser evil: the sign of how far social control reaches. There are people who escape from this control, who do not play by the rules. Thus, murders, robberies, rapes, terrorist acts often occur. However, all this is very far from constituting a problem comparable to mercantilism, authoritarianism, the *status quo* or repression. The second form of expression of the antisocial, which appears to us to be softer, is the violence in which exploitation takes place under the guise of socialness, in the bosom of institutions, sustaining a secret or explicitly exploiting power. I shall explain this through a situation from our remote past, though the symbiosis between the establishment and antisocialness is echoed today in the military-industrial-national complex.

There is a theory that the violent were the originators of masculine supremacy in our species. Many peoples have been studied, in which it is possible to reconstruct a certain progression: they become sedentary, they start to sow seeds, harvest, and have an agricultural surplus to store, and so no longer need to live day to day. Anthropologists affirm that the distribution of the agricultural surplus makes it necessary for someone to assume the function of the distributor and that primitive distributors were the most ancient chieftains. But distribution is not enough. The public treasury is something that must be looked after, and thugs surround the chieftain in order to fulfill their policing function. It is easy to imagine that in a culture in which the chieftains with an aggressive character are important the idea may arise of going to the neighboring village to take some of their provisions, particularly if there has been an affront, but also by virtue of a group spirit that enjoys fighting and exhibiting its strength. And, of course, when the danger exists of being attacked by a neighbor who thinks the same way, the contingent of guards has to be reinforced... and so we have the origin of the army.

The American anthropologist, Marvin Harris, who has collected a great deal of data on diverse cultures, cites the phrase of a native—of one of the Polynesian cultures, I believe—that is the echo of the epithet of the ancient chieftains: "great slayers of men and pigs." The expression suggests a mentality for which the sacrificing of animals and people is more or less the same thing; the mentality of those who have the trade of slaying, the tough guys. This might be the original development of what subsequently led to innumerable outrages in the history that we know.

Nowadays, there are historians who think that slavery was originally the slavery of women, because when a village was sacked, everything was razed to the ground and the men were killed, but the best was carried off: the women, domestic and reproductive female servants. Such was the attitude of these valiant tough guys. Later, of course, it occurred to them that they could also enslave the men.

I would say that this character—sadistic, tough, that tends towards the antisocial—has been highly determinant in the male dominance of our civilization. This has brought with it a great many problems—starting with the inner imbalance of the individual psyche, the repression of emotions and rationalism, having a bearing on things that have apparently nothing to do with masculinity but are the result of living with the masculine analytical half of our brain.

I have spoken of archaic times in reference to how "the system" has been based on power. But power nowadays is not in the hands of thugs with big muscles; we do not need such insensitive folk when we have cannons and missiles and when we have learned massively to desensitize ourselves. We do not need generals with a sadistic character, since killing has become an everyday event.

As the policing organ of civilization, the military organ, is intrinsic to its structure, we do not notice that it has grown in a cancerous way. In 1920, the North American military budget was one per cent of productivity, and by 1995 it was already more than fifty per cent. How much does the defense from the other barbarians who might cut off our heads consume! This explains much of the suffering and trouble in life in contemporary society.

In spite of its high technology, of the increase in productivity, of automatization, of the improvements in agriculture and in the exploitation of natural resources to their limits, there is still hunger and poverty as a result of the diversion of human resources towards the upkeep of armies and the manufacture of armaments.

DEPENDENCE

We have covered a large part of the enneagram of society. Let us now see the lower part, point IV. On the individual plane, we are dealing with the envy that each carries inside: that feeling of not being much, that longing intensely for something that is out there, a "give me, give me," a sense of frustration. It is clear that this also exists on the collective plane. A German sociologist— Helmet Schoek[2]—has written a book about envy in which he proposes that it is no less true to say that envy moves the world than to say—like Freud—that what moves the

---

[2]Helmut Schoek, *Envy: A Theory of Social Behaviour*. Indianapolis, 1987, The Liberty Fund.

world is the libido. What tells us more about society, sexuality or competition, the desire to have what others have? It is debatable.

Just as those in whom this passion is very strong usually renounce their needs at the same time as they ardently desire that which they renounce, thus feeling resentment, on the collective plane there are groups that are more oppressed than others, because they characterologically tend towards submission, though they harbor a resentment that is proportional to the oppression they suffer.

Half the world forms an oppressive system and the other half an oppressed system, and this is also an organic part of society that is related to a compulsively servile aspect of the human character. This feature is found more in the female sex, that says "amen" to the other, and for this reason Aristophanes, in a play called *Lysistrata*, dreamt that women could come to an agreement to refuse to have sex with their husbands and thus prevent wars. Is not woman's contribution to each of our homes sufficiently important for a universal strike to have possible repercussions in the running of the world? I would say that this idea has been implicitly taken up by feminism, which has pushed women to take on a political function. We may expect the sensibility and way of thinking of women to begin to be reflected in the running of world affairs. The fact that excessively subjugated women all over the world have decided to protest, cry out, and demand their rights is a massive phenomenon with great social repercussions.

It would be unjust to say that the oppressed are as much to blame as the oppressors or that the downtrodden are as much to blame as those who ride roughshod over them. But nowadays, in the North American world, the word "codependency" is heard a lot, referring both to those who possess a deficient character and overdepend on exploiters, and to the exploiters who depend on those who let themselves be exploited. In other words, dependency is relevant in social discourse and not only to the individual, and there is a need for each person gradually to become more autonomous. In a certain sense, the cure—individual evolution—supposes the passage from an excessively dependent position to a more autonomous one. If we achieved this on a massive scale, we would have a less exploitative society.

ASOCIALNESS AND ANOMIE

Point V, next to point IV, corresponds to a character that is also closer to the exploited than to exploiters: the "schizoid" character, those who "look as if butter wouldn't melt in their mouths," the weak. This is an impotent character, in the sense of having very little capacity to do, to move things. These are people who when faced with any kind of effort feel that it is not worth it, that "it's not going to work out for me." On the social plane, this impotence contributes to things staying as they are. I come from a country, Chile, in which this character is very common, and this leads to stagnation. People do not dare to take on commitments because they feel that this does not lead anywhere.

What social pathology is associated with this form of being in the world that is more a case of *not* being in this world? The ailment of those who feel that they are not here and those who are the observers of the world, a species of extraterrestrials who are waiting for the show to end.

A sociological manifestation of this is what E.

Durkheim, in his study on suicide, called *anomie*: what occurs when a person dissociates so much that he or she loses the meaning of life. This occurs a lot with beggars, with isolated people who, as they do not have sufficient social ties, lose their system of values; values that always require a relationship, that have to be fed by contact with the world, that have to be nourished by interaction with others. Otherwise, they grow old. And then the person who is in the world without being of it starts to feel: "What for? I don't believe in anything, nothing matters at all, life has no meaning."

We live in an age in which the neurosis of meaninglessness abounds. Many people suffer from this, something which in ancient times did not occur, or at least was not noteworthy. An existentialist, Viktor Frankl, was the one who coined the term "neurosis of meaninglessness." It was a novelty, it had occurred to nobody until then that many people suffered from this affliction. Today it is an ill that affects almost everyone, since even quite social people have a relatively superficial sociability and share the intimate loneliness of the schizoid. We are losing the relationship with our neighbor; we do not live family relationships as the ancients used to; we do not have a sense of community comparable with that of other ages; there is no public life like before; we are much more isolated; we are more individualistic; and to the extent that we are emptier, we have lost meaning. The modern world is cold, scientific, mechanical, and abstract. All these ills of society have been well caricatured in the film *Dr. Strangelove*, in which Peter Sellers, a mad professor, is about to press a button and destroy the world. This is a completely rational and cold mentality, like that of our world, more indifferent each day.

170

CORRUPTION AND THE LIGHT ATTITUDE

We have the social projections of two more characters left to examine. The character of EVII is that of a person who does not seem to suffer as much as the others; a happy character, who has a good time, who believes in nothing. EVIIs would appear to be removed from the ills of the world, as they are anticonventional and critical. Nearly always on the edge of society, in the modern world this type may be embodied by the hippie, and in bygone days by the "priest-hater," though EVII may be a utopian idealist as well as a friendly bandit like Aladdin, whom Walt Disney Studios managed to portray as a charming petty thief who feels less virtuous than his petty peers in a world in which injustice justifies a certain degree of transgression. This character may also be an excessively accommodating individual who lives off the system like a parasite. A Spanish psychiatrist[3] has given this type a name: *light* man. We are in the age of the *light* man, a good-time consumer; an individualist who cares about nothing at all; a hedonist. Many people may think: "What's so bad about that?," as if the sin of gluttony—with which this character is associated—were not as serious as other sins, given that pleasure is not as destructive as violence or cruelty.

But among the ills of the world there is one which is fairly serious, that has to do precisely with this *light* attitude: corruption. If one believes in nothing, if one implicitly thinks that authority is of no use, that the system is corrupted, then one must do what is the most convenient for oneself. And with many people like that, it is impossible for the collective to function.

---

[3]Enrique Rojas, *El hombre light,* Temas de Hoy, Madrid, 1992.

When Socrates was offered the chance to flee, he preferred to give his life as an example of support for the ideal of democracy, to reinforce the belief in the idea that the people may govern themselves; that even if they make a mistake, a system may in principal be reached in which wisdom reigns. How far we are today from this attitude! We all think, to a greater or lesser degree, that governments are of no use to anyone and that tax returns can be fiddled, because... what does it matter, if nothing functions! The EVII character is more critical and individualistic than the others; but this act of individualism, which could be understood as a love for oneself (or a love for a friend, when it is a friend who is done a favor), does nonetheless have destructive consequences for the collective. I am speaking about corruption. Some "scam" is done so that someone receives another payment, or an international loan is applied for that the country does not need so that ten per cent ends up in the hands of so and so. Something similar occurs in my country, which nowadays is up to its neck in debt, just like in other South American countries: it is of interest to certain individuals to support this economic policy of receiving loans from large foreign banks and to spend more than what is produced.

It may be said that, among the ills of the world, corruption is no less significant than the rest. There are countries that have truly entered into crisis because of it, like Brazil, where EVII abounds, or Italy, where the combination of anti-socialness and the gang-pack spirit is also very notorious (think, for example, how much "love for the family" the Mafia entails). However, I believe that more important than illegal corruption in the course of history (and no less in our day and age) has been a corruption that is unknown to the law but which uses the law as a weapon as well as a shield. Let us call it the *intrinsic* corruption of the system.

When oppression adulterates and disturbs the healthy, brotherly relationships between human beings, it entails a corrupt authority, and the system that we call "civilization" (which commenced with the taking of power by the males of our species in the Bronze Age) is a system that is not only injust but also corrupt. It hides behind rhetoric and the media via false ideals and pretended virtue.

If corruption is a response to injustice it may also be said that it perpetuates injustice—particularly when delinquency becomes part of the system.

Historians have written extensively about the corruption of the popes and the church as well as the corruption unleashed by temporal power—whether it be tyrannical, monarchic, or "democratic." But perhaps nowadays the corruption of the business world is more important, since our times are characterized by the submission of political power to economic power. Thus, it may be that the implicit and perhaps sometimes unconscious preferential attention to private profit over the consideration of what is good for everyone by those who run the organization of global business is the cause of more pain in the present-day world than the sum of the crimes of those who inhabit the prisons.

FALSE LOVE

There is another character that resembles this one: the proud character, EII, which is neither so oppressive nor so oppressed. Like EVII, it is a pseudo-social character more than a social one: social, in name only, and antisocial, in a hidden way. The proud character, like the envious character, is represented much more in the female sex. Part of the contingent of the world's women is a subjugated contingent; their attitude of excessive renouncement, their service, is extendable to the world's servants in general. On the other hand, we find triumphant women, who know how to live at the side of "the beast" (power) and how to take advantage of it. The femme fatale is so irresistible, so charming, that she is forgiven all. She is like a parasite on society. (There are ants that have parasites almost their same size; they live hanging from them and when the ant is going to eat, the parasite takes its food and puts it into its own mouth.) But if Aristophanes had fixed his attention on them, he would perhaps have defended them by saying that they also contribute to the running of world affairs.

I think that the best symbol of all this is the one we find at the end of St. John's Apocalypse, when the Great Beast appears and the Great Whore, corresponding with the city (the whore) that sells itself to the Great Beast. The city is made up of human beings, and we human beings are selling ourselves to brute power, to the power of the system. Some individuals—especially if they have this proud character, so widely represented in the female half of the world—even sell themselves. If men are cowards, women are specialists in exchanging pleasure for a quiet life at the side of power. They say to the Great Beast: "You are more powerful than me, but you give me enough to take me in your carriage." It might be said that this so very generalized seductive love also contributes to the global running of society, since we all succumb to it and since its arts are highly developed and perfected. Although they do not appear in any book, nor are they an institution, these arts blind us to the nature of love. And so we are ignorant of the fundamental sickness of love—the error concerning what love is—which is like a great plague that perpetuates itself down through the generations and that creates other problems.

BY WAY OF CONCLUSION

With this, the "softest" and most charming of pathologies, I have finished the journey around the enneagram of society. It only remains for me to present some general overall observations.

If we look panoramically at the sphere of capital social pathologies, we see that those characters situated at the vertices of the triangle of the Enneagram, as well as the neighboring points to IX (sociocultural inertia), find their institutional echo in the world, constituting its *establishment.* We may talk of the social system that the "patriarchal system" as a whole supposes: a corrupted military-industrial-bureaucratic-financial complex that has turned more and more against life.

The points that remain outside correspond to the ends of the lines that join V to VII and IV to II, on the left and right of the Enneagram, respectively. What stands out is the fact that although the character pathologies in these positions correspond to social pathologies, the pseudo-social characters (VII and II), and those that correspond to the "poor of spirit" (IV and V)—at the bottom of the Enneagram—have a special relationship with the forces of renovation that are arising in our age.

Points II and IV, together on the right wing of the Enneagram, correspond to female characters, and given the fact that the millenial character of our establishment is patriarchal, a great deal may be expected from the actual process of balancing of the sexes. The political balance between both will surely contribute to balancing our inner world, the family world of the generations to come—and vice versa. The moment the family evolves from a quasi-tyrannical model to a heterarchical structure of beings that relate to one another healthily, we shall have taken the most significant step—I believe—towards a democratic and balanced political world.

On the other hand, points V and VII, on the left, have to do with information, since schizoid characters devote themselves to the acquisition of knowledge and oral-optimists to communication. Experts on social change say that the great change in our age (the "third wave" that Toffler spoke of, which he compares in importance with the revolution of the neolithic period) is that which has developed in the information sphere, a power that has entered into competition with the *anciens régimes*. The world cannot stay the same with the information we now possess, since just as the truth is liberating for the individual, so knowledge can cure us of myths and collective superstitions, as well as of the inertia of the system itself. Hence the theme of the ills of the world seems to me to be worthy of this exploration; to remedy them, as in the case of the ills of the soul, we need to know them.

Perhaps the ills of the world constitute the most modern of themes, despite the fact that since time immemorial, even prehistoric times, the world has functioned fairly badly. Our species has had an unfortunate life right from its beginnings. In the ice ages, we had to earn our living "cracking our neighbors' skulls," and since then we are somewhat callused. Although we now notice this less, thanks to habituation, I believe that deep down the political life of nations is still a life of head-hunters, albeit highly justified and rationalized. There are ideologies that make us feel that this is normal.

After so many attempts to fix the world, after so many reforms and political systems, it seems to me that we, in this post-modern age, are reaching the collapse of ideologies. Now no one believes in anything. And to a certain extent this is all right, since many ideas have been presented in a manipulative way, with ulterior motives. In the current search for solutions to global problems, an excessively technical attitude stands out, which neglects the human aspect of the question.

Many futurists tell us that we are running the risk of destroying ourselves, and there exists a great chance that this may be so. With the progressive increase in the population, social struggles will result not only in mutual violence, but also in the destruction of flora and fauna, as well as the exhaustion of resources that the planet provides to us. There are several possible scenarios, and each day the decisive role of the human factor is invoked. I think that the world is the product of what we carry within us. And hence the hypothesis that the ills of society are the result and amplification of our (scarcely acknowledged) incapacity to maintain healthy relationships is worthy of special attention.

If we consider it difficult for a healthy society to exist without the foundation of healthy individuals, it becomes imperative to recognize the political value of individual transformation; though this transformation can hardly be promoted by existing institutions. What is called education has nothing to do with education (it is more an irrelevant information machine), and public health has hardly anything to do with emotional health.

It would give me great satisfaction if this essay has

served as an effective invitation to you to think about all that will be added unto us if we first of all occupy the kingdom that is to be found within our hearts.

Glossary

Altruistic self-sacrifice: A defense mechanism by means of which the person interferes with the knowledge of his or her needs and desires through an excessively generous and obliging attitude.

Amorous "cannibalism": Allowing oneself to be carried by the intensity of the thirst for love towards an "amorous" relationship that is voracious or devouring.

Borderline personality: A disturbance of personality characterized by mood swings, destructive behavior, irritability, and low self-esteem.

Chakra: Literally "circle," also translated as "center of energy." One or other of the points along the central axis of the body considered in Eastern esoteric traditions to be part of the subtle or energy body that is experienced at certain levels on the path of spiritual development.

Character: The set of habits, ways of thinking and feeling that have been conditioned during childhood. Spiritual psychologists consider this to be a "small self" as opposed to the true self, the ego or personality as opposed to the essence of the mind, the soul, the central nucleus.

Character neurosis: A neurosis that does not manifest as subjective symptoms like anxiety or depression, but rather as a disturbed way of behaving.

Contraphobic: The person who instead of retreating when faced with fear "flees forward," and defends him or herself by attacking.

Cyclothymic: A character described by Kretschmer as sociable, friendly, expansive, cheerful, and phlegmatic, though susceptible to manic-depressive states.

Defense mechanisms: A series of processes through which the individual maintains certain thoughts, perceptions, emotions, or impulses that threaten his or her well being or "ideal" image.

Egocentric generosity: An apparently generous attitude, but one that is secretly and unconsciously selfish, common in people with a great need for attention.

Enneagram: A geometric figure with nine points that are related in a particular way. Considered a symbol of certain cosmic laws, especially that of the ternary structure of the universe and consciousness, as well as that of the septenary cyclical progression of the future, also called the "Law of the Octave."

Enneatype: Type of character or style of personality in accordance with the enneagram.

Extrinsic orientation (D. Riesman): A concept that is applied to people who are predominantly guided by the conduct, opinions, and values of their surroundings.

Fantastic pseudology: The name given in the past to the most exaggerated form of a disposition to lie and to invent events that do not exist.

Formation reactive: A defense mechanism described by Freud in "A Sexual Theory" and other essays, due to which a person ignores his or her impulse and disguises it as its opposite (forbidden sexuality and aggression are typically disguised as excessive moralism).

Gestalt therapy: School of psychotherapy founded by Fritz Perls that stresses concentration on the present, the use of dramatization, the integration of sub-personalities, authenticity, and the suspension of compulsive thought.

Histrionic: See *histrionic disorder*.

Histrionic disorder: A high degree of emotionality and a desire to attract attention. When this desire is frustrated, the person may make a scene. This type of neurotic personality is also characterized by an exaggeration of the tendency to provoke and seduce.

Hysteroid: The set of personality styles in which seductiveness, expressivity, and theatricality predominate.

Identification with the aggressor: Anna Freud gives this name to the defense mechanism by means of which a person makes the characteristics of an aggressively reprehensive authority his or her own, thus becoming his or her own enemy.

Marketing orientation: Fromm says of this that its fundamental feature is the presentation of oneself in the "personality marketplace," which likewise entails a tendency to conform to the way of thinking or models of success that are in fashion.

Masochism: In a broad sense, a character disposition according to which a person adopts a position of suffering, tends to allow him or herself to become a victim in order to expiate his or her lack of merit, and attempts, at the same time, to attain love through the level of need and frustration (commonly expressed through moaning and complaining).

Metaproblem: A formulation of a problem situation such that the diverse problems that make this up are considered to be derived from a basic phenomenon at a deeper level.

Narcissism: As opposed to love for another, this is "love" towards an idealized image of oneself.

Neurosis: In the broadest sense, a condition of emotional disturbance and limited awareness that is usually considered "normal" due to it being almost universally shared.

Neurotic motivation: As opposed to healthy motivation, which is loving, neurotic motivation creates—as Maslow has pointed out—a "deficit": it does not lead to overabundance and a brimming over, but rather seeks satisfaction that is not attained.

Neurotic needs: As opposed to instinctive needs, neurotic needs are insatiable and antievolutionary. According to the theory expounded here, the "passions" of protoanalysis are the equivalent of basic neurotic needs.

Obsessive disorder: The DSM-IV talks of a pattern that comprehends preoccupation with order, perfectionism and control, both mental and interpersonal, all at the expense of flexibility, openness and even efficiency.

Oral optimistic: Characterized by exaggerated optimism, generosity, social sparkle, anxiety to have everything, and a great need to communicate; the type of person who likes to listen to him or herself.

Paranoid disorder: What the DSM-IV calls "paranoid disorder of the personality" corresponds to the most aggressive form adopted by mistrust. These people see exploitation, hurt, or deception where there is none; they feel insulted or slandered by the world and react to this with indignation.

Permissiveness: An open attitude, sometimes too indulgent, towards one's own impulses or the satisfaction of the desires of others.

Personality: A word that has been used in diverse senses. In this book, it is the equivalent of character and also of the ego of the transpersonalists—our apparent, conditioned identity.

Phallic narcissist: A type of character described by Wilhelm Reich characterized by being domineering, overbearing, daring, impulsive, and brazen.

Projection: The attributing to others of one's own unconscious emotions, thoughts, or intentions.

Projective identification: A term proposed by Melanie Klein for a mechanism which expresses itself in fantasies and in which the subject projects, in an imaginary way, a part of oneself into another person with the intention of hurting or controlling that person.

Protoanalysis: The name given by Oscar Ichazo to the body of knowledge that he transmitted concerning personality analysis in the light of the enneagram.

Psychodynamics: Clarification of the motivational background that drives actions, emotions, and thoughts. Classic psychoanalysis identified this background with the instinctive, and the school of Kleinian object relations with a basic interpersonal drive. In my work *Character and Neurosis*, I introduced the concept of "existential psychodynamics," according to which passions and fixations arise from a loss of awareness of being.

Psychopathy: The name "psychopathic disorder" has been given to a type of disorder that characteristically does not cause the individual, but rather others, suffering.

Psychosis: Madness.

Retroflection: A term introduced by Fritz Perls to refer to the turning against oneself of an impulse originally aimed at another.

Schizoid: See *schizoid disorder*.

Schizoid disorder: What is characteristic in individuals who suffer from this disorder is a distancing from social relationships and the limited expression of emotions in the interpersonal context. It is, in short, a disorder of the solitary.

Self-demonization: Seeing oneself—in a condemnatory way—as evil.

Self-invalidation: Giving less value, merit or credibility to one's own experiences or actions.

Zoroastrian: A follower of the religion of Zoroaster (Zarathustra) (628-551 B.C.), a visionary who was the original spiritual teacher of the Persians or Magi.

Dear Reader of *The Enneagram of Society*

For a current catalog, including a variety of books, audio and video recordings of Claudio Naranjo, you may contact Gateways at the address below with no obligation to purchase.

Gateways Books and Tapes
P.O. Box 370-ENS
Nevada City, CA 95959
(800) 869-0658 or (530) 477-8101
www.gatewaysbooksandtapes.com
email: info@gatewaysbooksandtapes.com

Other Gateways Consciousness Classics
by Claudio Naranjo:

Ennea-type Structures
Self Analysis for the Seeker
This book is filled with the wisdom distilled from years of working with people in the context of psychospiritual growth practices...
Ralph Metzner, Ph.D.
Author of *The Unfolding Self*

The Divine Child and the Hero
Inner Meaning in Children's Literature
In writing this book, Claudio Naranjo has submitted himself to what the I-Ching calls "The Taming Power of the Small." I feel certain that his eight authors, whether they are in this world or in Heaven, will salute Dr. Naranjo for this perceptive essay.
from the preface by P.L. Travers, author of *Mary Poppins*